Better Phonics and Beyond in

Phonics Fun for Kids and Parents on the Go

Lisa Deters

Series Editor: Mark Pennington

PRIMA PUBLISHING

3000 Lava Ridge Court • Roseville, California 95661

(800) 632-8676 • www.primalifestyles.com

The 5 MINUTES A DAY logo is a trademark of Prima Communications, Inc. PRIMA PUBLISHING and colophon are trademarks of Prima Communications Inc., registered with the United States Patent and Trademark Office.

Interior illustrations by Susan Sugnet

Library of Congress Cataloging-in-Publication Data
Deters, Lisa.
    Better phonics and beyond in 5 minutes a day : phonics fun for kids and parents on the go / Lisa Deters.
       p. cm. — (5 minutes a day series)
    Includes index.
    ISBN 0-7615-2428-2
    1. Reading--Phonetic method. 2. Reading--Parent participation. 3. English language--Orthography and spelling--Study and teaching (Elementary) I. Title. II. Series.
LB1573.3 .D48 2001
372.46'5—dc21   00-052876

01 02 03 04 II 10 9 8 7 6 5 4 3 2 1
Printed in the United States of America

How to Order

Single copies may be ordered from Prima Publishing, 3000 Lava Ridge Court, Roseville, CA 95661; telephone (800) 632-8676, ext. 4444. Quantity discounts are also available. On your letterhead, include information concerning the intended use of the books and the number of books you wish to purchase.

Visit us online at www.primalifestyles.com

I dedicate this book to my three sons, Daniel, Brian, and Jason.
You are everything to me. I love you.

Contents

Acknowledgments

I would like to acknowledge some people who played an important role in helping to create this book. First, I would like to thank Jamie Miller at Prima for giving me the opportunity to write this book and Mark Pennington for his work as Series Editor. A special acknowledgment is given to Tara Mead for her book production expertise and final editing support. I am grateful for the support of my peers, the Elk Grove Reading Specialists, who share so openly their ideas and successes and who have allowed me to become a better reading teacher simply by association. I am also grateful for the support of my supervisor, Karen Hayashi, who consistently provides learning opportunities. By sharing her ideas and philosophies, she has become a driving force helping me to improve my own teaching practices. I thank Joseph Adrienne for encouraging me to face new challenges. And finally, but always first in my heart, I thank my family for their love and support.

Introduction

When children learn to read, they are launched into a world of written information and limitless opportunities. Carefully planned phonics instruction is crucial for developing the skills that children need to become good readers. Children who do not have basic phonics skills struggle to become good readers. They are at a great disadvantage. Not only do they have more limited opportunities to learn, but also their day-to-day reading tasks become more challenging.

Better Phonics and Beyond in 5 Minutes a Day is designed to help parents teach phonics to their intermediate-age children. Over the years, studies have shown that children who have a solid mastery of phonics are more successful in reading and spelling. This book has everything that you need to help your child understand the relationships between sounds and letters, develop the ability to distinguish sounds, and read these letter patterns.

Unlike other phonics workbooks, this book actually teaches you *how* best to help your child learn phonics without all the teacher jargon. It follows a flexible, user-friendly approach that allows you to pick any activity whenever you have an extra five minutes with your child. The clear instructions and fun interactive word games will equip you with practical strategies to help your child develop the skills needed to sound out unfamiliar words accurately and effortlessly. These strategies will help you teach critical reading skills and concepts even if you lack prior teaching experience or lengthy preparation.

Each teaching lesson starts with a Parents' Corner that contains exactly what you need to provide effective, high-quality instruction with a limited time commitment. Each lesson also includes Teaching Tips that will give you quick ideas for explaining the sometimes complicated ideas of phonics.

Lessons use three types of activities to help your child gain mastery of phonics. At the Kitchen Table activities are for you and your child to work through together whenever you have a few minutes to spare at home. Often these activities require this book or manipulatives, such as flashcards or paper and pencil. These activities give you and your child the chance to practice each phonics concept together. On the Go activities can be done while you are running errands, driving to school, or even doing the dishes. Rather than carrying the book around everywhere you go, simply read through the activity before heading out the door, and use it to make the time go faster while waiting in line or driving to the doctor's office. Finally, the On Your Own activities provide additional practice for your child to extend learning on his or her own time. All of these activities are fun, quick, and easy to understand.

Some words present a challenge to the beginning reader because they cannot be sounded out correctly using the basic phonics rules. We refer to these words as "sight words," and readers must learn to identify them rapidly when they see them. The best way to practice these sight words is to make them into flashcards and practice a few each night. Once your child is able to identify them all, try for a speed record. As children increase their sight word vocabulary, they are able to read faster and more accurately, as well as with more confidence. A list of sight words appropriate to the level of instruction are introduced at the end of each chapter. In addition, each chapter ends with a check-up so you and your child can review what has been learned in that chapter.

In this book, to help distinguish between the sounds and letters of our language, italic type refers to a sound while letters in quotation marks refer to the letters themselves. For example, short *a* and ă both represent the short vowel sound of the letter "a." Likewise, quotation marks are used around word parts, such as prefixes ("pre"), while italics are used for whole words (*pretend*).

The strategies in this book will complement any teaching approach used in your child's school. The emphasis is on identifying your child's strengths and weaknesses, and then providing the specific instructional activities, games, and practice opportunities that will appropriately challenge your child. Using these skills, your child will become a faster, more accurate, and more confident reader.

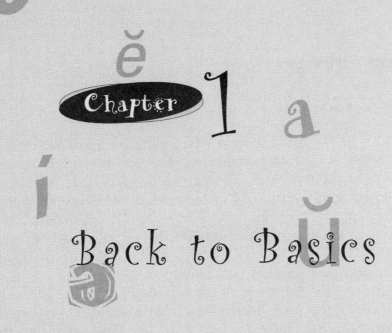

Chapter 1

Back to Basics

In This Chapter

- Alphabet Review
- The Wonderful World of Short Vowels
- Consonant Teams
- The Magic "e"
- Soft Sounds and Hard Sounds
- Sight Words and Check-Up

ALPHABET REVIEW

Parents' Corner

Phonics skills are the building blocks of reading. Each new skill builds on those before it. The consonant and short vowel sounds are the building blocks for the more complicated phonics that will follow. When children don't gain a solid understanding of these critical concepts, many struggle when asked to read more difficult material. Use the activities in this chapter to review basic phonics skills with your child.

The English language has only twenty-six letters, but more than forty separate sounds. Single consonant sounds are the easiest to learn because, most of the time, their sounds are predictably consistent. When saying letter sounds, make sure your child does not distort the sound by adding the *uh* sound, such as *tuh* for *t* or *buh* for *b*. That way, your child won't experience the confusion that is often caused by the unnecessary *uh* sound. Example: *s-ă-t* is correct, but *suh-ă-tuh* is not.

The upside down "e" (ə) is called *schwa*. In words, it may be represented by any of the vowel letters. In the Sound Off! review, this sound is represented by the letter "u."

Your intermediate-age child will benefit from a solid review of the basic skills of letter and sound recognition. Starting with the basics will help support many of the more advanced phonics skills found later in *Better Phonics and Beyond in 5 Minutes a Day* lessons.

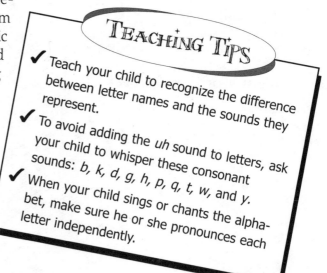

TEACHING TIPS

✔ Teach your child to recognize the difference between letter names and the sounds they represent.

✔ To avoid adding the *uh* sound to letters, ask your child to whisper these consonant sounds: *b, k, d, g, h, p, q, t, w,* and *y*.

✔ When your child sings or chants the alphabet, make sure he or she pronounces each letter independently.

AT THE KITCHEN TABLE

SOUND OFF!

Look at the list that follows. Can you say the names and the sounds for all the letters in the alphabet? Put a check by any letter you have trouble with. Then you will know which letters you need to practice more. After you go through the list once by yourself, have your parent listen as you read through it again. Are there any other letters that you need to practice some more?

Say the Letter	Say the Sound	Say the Word	
A-a	ă	alligator	
B-b	b	ball	
C-c	k	cat	
D-d	d	duck	
E-e	ĕ	elephant	
F-f	f	frog	

G-g	*g*	grapes	
H-h	*h*	hog	
I-i	*ĭ*	igloo	
J-j	*j*	jam	
K-k	*k*	kangaroo	
L-l	*l*	lamb	
M-m	*m*	marbles	
N-n	*n*	nest	
O-o	*ŏ*	octopus	

P-p	*p*	pen
Q-q	*k*	quail
R-r	*r*	rain
S-s	*s*	sink
T-t	*t*	tub
U-u	*ŭ*	umbrella
V-v	*v*	vase
W-w	*w*	watch
X-x	*ks*	xylophone

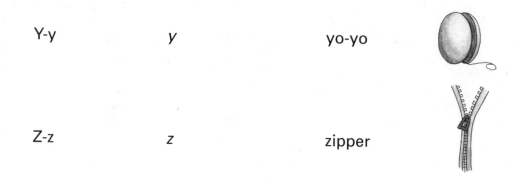

Y-y	*y*	yo-yo
Z-z	*z*	zipper

On Your Own

LOOK OUT FOR THE B'S!

Ask your parent for a colorful advertising page from the newspaper or a magazine. Choose a letter from the alphabet and write it at the top of the page. Let's say you choose the letter "b." Read through the page and circle every "b" that you see. Did you find them all? How many different colors and styles of the letter "b" did you find? Ask for a new page and look for another letter this time.

CONSONANT PICTURE DICTIONARY

Make a picture dictionary of things that begin with the consonants. Remember, consonants are any letters that aren't vowels. You can use ideas from the Sound Off! exercise on pages 3–6 and any consonants you circled in the newspaper or magazine pages above. Make one page for each letter. Be creative and draw the pictures yourself or cut them out of magazines—remember to ask permission first!

IMAGINE THAT!

The 5 vowels make 20 different sounds in English. The other 21 letters (consonants) make 25 separate sounds. Almost 50 percent of the sounds used in English are made from only 5 letters.

On the Go. . .

GUESS AGAIN!

In this game, you say a category and several letters, and your child must think of words in that category that begin with those letters. For example, you say: "The category is sports. Tell me the name of three sports—one that begins with a B, one that begins with an H, and one that begins with an F." Your child then has to think of sports that begin with these letters. Maybe baseball, hockey, and football. Take turns thinking of categories. Here are a few to help you get started: food, colors, football teams, television shows, names of family or friends, book titles, music groups, cartoon characters, or states. This is a great way for children to become comfortable with the relationship between letters and sounds.

INVENT A SILLY STORY

In this game, take turns telling parts of a story, one sentence at a time, inventing the story as you go along. The tricky part is that the first word in each sentence must begin with the next letter of the alphabet. This is a fun game to play with two, three, or more players. Here is an example of how one story began:

A boy and his friend were walking to school. Before too long they found something weird. Carefully the boy picked it up. "Don't pick that up," said his friend.

THE WONDERFUL WORLD OF SHORT VOWELS

Parents' Corner

Many parents ask, "How do I know where to begin helping my child?" Start by asking your child's teacher what concepts and activities your child is learning at school, and then ask how well your child is performing in these activities. This will give you a place to start. Complete the phonics review activities in this chapter to see which basic phonics skills your child has mastered. This information will help you determine where to focus your efforts. Remember, a child must learn consonant and short vowel sounds before he or she can become a successful reader.

TEACHING TIPS

✓ Give your child some examples of short vowel words: *pan, hen, kick, hot, fun.* Take turns adding to this list.

✓ Short vowel sounds can be tricky because they change as they are affected by other letters. Compare *hen* with *help.*

✓ Help your child practice listening to and repeating the sounds in this lesson.

The vowels in our alphabet can have many different sounds. The sound a vowel makes depends on whether it is followed by a consonant or another vowel, stands alone, or is followed by a final "e." Vowel sounds are usually made with the mouth in an open position. By paying attention to the shape of the mouth, your child can master the short vowel sounds. Review the short vowel rule with your child.

Short Vowel Rule

When a word or a syllable has one vowel, and the vowel is not at the end of the word, the vowel sound is usually short. Short *a* makes the ă in *alligator* sound, short *e* makes the ĕ in *elephant* sound, short *i* makes the ĭ in *igloo* sound, short *o* makes the ŏ in *octopus* sound, and short *u* makes the ŭ in *umbrella* sound.

AT THE KITCHEN TABLE

READY, SET, REVIEW

Make new words by writing the vowel listed at the top of each column in each blank space in that column. Read the words in each row to yourself. Now say the words out loud and ask your parent to check you out. Did you pronounce them all right?

a	e	i	o	u
1. b__t	**2.** h__n	**3.** w__n	**4.** d__g	**5.** c__b
6. t__p	**7.** n__t	**8.** p__g	**9.** kn__ck	**10.** r__n
11. p__n	**12.** b__lt	**13.** sw__m	**14.** p__t	**15.** t__b

Now look at the columns below. Figure out where each of the words above should be placed in the table below. Can any words be used in more than one column?

Things You Can Do	Kinds of Animals	Things You Can Use

On the Go...

THE SOUND MATCHING GAME

Short vowel sounds can be very tricky for your child. One great way to practice hearing the difference between vowel sounds is to play the Sound Matching Game. Say a word with a short vowel sound and name the vowel and its sound. For example, you might say "Cat: The vowel is 'a,' and the sound is ă." Then have your child pick another word with the same vowel sound, such as bat. Keep taking turns until you or your child can't think of another word with the same sound. Then pick a different short vowel and play again.

On Your Own

LET'S GO ON A HUNT

Go on a hunt for short vowel sounds. You'll need a pencil and a pad of Post-it Notes or some other sticky paper. Hunt for the items in your room that have short vowel sounds. For each item, write the short vowel letter on the Post-it Note and stick it to the item. Be sure you have a lot of these sticky papers ready. For example, you would place a Post-it Note with the letter "e" on your bed. Once you finish labeling everything in your room, ask your parents if you can continue in the living room!

Just for Fun!

What two letters of the alphabet contain nothing?
MT!

CONSONANT TEAMS

Parents' Corner

When two or more consonants are placed together in a word, they often stand for one sound. These consonant teams, which are also called *consonant digraphs*, are "th," "ch," "tch," "sh," "ng," and "wh." Let's look at each combination separately.

- The letters "th" make two different sounds. One sound is heard in *this, these,* and *there.* The other sound is heard in *three, things,* and *threw.*
- The letters "ch" make the *ch* sound heard in *chair, bench,* and *teach.* The letters "ch" also make the *k* sound as in *Christine* and the *sh* sound as in *Charlotte.* These are not the common sounds associated with the consonant pair "ch," but your child needs to know that there are exceptions to these rules.
- The combination "tch" makes the *ch* sound heard in *watch, catch, switch,* and *match.* The letters "tch" are found only at the end of a word.
- The "sh" pair makes the *sh* sound heard in *short, shirt, wash,* and *brush.*
- The "ng" pair makes the *ng* sound heard in *ring, gong, bang,* and *lung.*
- The "wh" pair makes the *wh* sound heard in *when, where, why,* and *what.* The letters "wh" are found only at the beginning of a word.

TEACHING TIPS

✓ Help your child hear how the individual sounds of each letter in a consonant team are replaced by only one sound.

✓ Teach your child to correctly pronounce each of the consonant team sounds.

✓ For each combination, ask your child to say the sound aloud and then think of a word that contains that sound.

AT THE KITCHEN TABLE

SENSE OR NONSENSE?

In the sentences below, fill in the blanks with one of the words that follow it. Choose the word that best completes each sentence.

1. Tom needs a new _____ for his paint set.

         switch   branch   brush

2. She looked at the time on her new _____.

         watch   batch   peach

3. Do not walk on _____ ice.

         cheat   thread   thin

4. Matt _____ the wood with his axe.

    shopped   whipped   chopped

5. The girl gave her dog a _____.

         teeth   sheet   bath

6. I like to sit on a _____ when I go to the park.

    tooth   witch   bench

7. Harry ate a _____ slice of turkey.

       scratch   chunk   thick

8. My bike needs a new _____.

       sheep   when   wheel

9. A heavy chain keeps the gate _____.

       chops   three   shut

10. A _____ is my favorite fruit.

   peach   splash   path

Ask your parent to listen to you read each sentence out loud. Did you pick the best answer every time? If you did, give yourself a pat on the back (or let your parent do so).

On Your Own

COLORFUL CONSONANT PARTNERS

Ask your parents for some old magazines and six different colors of marking pens or crayons. Choose six pages and circle the words that have consonant teams, using a different color for each consonant group. For example, red for "ch" and blue for "sh." When you have finished, make a list of all the words you found. Then sort your list by beginning and ending sounds. Mark a "B" by each word that has a consonant team at the beginning, and an "E" by each word that has a consonant team at the end.

Just for Fun!

How do you spell hard water with just three letters?

Ice

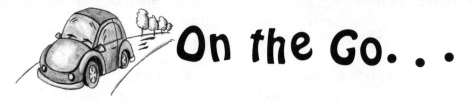

On the Go...

THUMBS UP, THUMBS DOWN

Choose a consonant team ("th," "ch," "tch," "sh," "ng," or "wh") and ask your child what sound it makes. Then say a word and have your child signal thumbs up if the consonant digraph is in the word or thumbs down if it is not. For example:

> I choose the letters "s" and "h." What sound do these letters make?

Your child should say *sh*. If not, help your child figure out what sound "s" and "h" make together. Once your child understands, continue with the activity. As you say the words, your child should give a thumbs up if the word has the consonant digraph and thumbs down if not. If you say *watch*, you get a thumbs down. If you say *fish*, you get a thumbs up. Continue with such words as *lunch* and *brush*. If your child finds this too easy, you can make it more challenging by using longer words.

THE MAGIC "E"

Parents' Corner

Ask your child to recite the long vowel sounds to be sure he or she can distinguish between long and short vowel sounds. Teach your child that long vowel sounds are the same as the letter name. That is, long *a* makes the $\bar{a}$ in *apron* sound, long *e* makes the $\bar{e}$ in *eagle* sound, long *i* makes the $\bar{i}$ in *ice* sound, long *o* makes the $\bar{o}$ in *ocean* sound, and long *u* makes the $\bar{u}$ in *Utah* sound.

Until now, a single letter, or a single set of letters, has represented a single sound. The final "e" rule represents a change in what your child has been learning. The final "e" is usually an inexperienced reader's first exposure to long vowel sounds. Review the Final "e" Rule with your child:

The Final "e" Rule
An "e" at the end makes the first vowel sound long.
If I remember this rule, I'll never go wrong.

Explain that the final "e" is like a signal to the nearest vowel, indicating whether the vowel will have a long or short sound. The final "e" can usually only signal past one letter. In *care*, for example, the final "e" signals that the "a" will be a long *a* sound. But in *nurse*, the final "e" does not signal past the "r" and "s," so the "u" is not a long *u* sound. The final "e" also functions as the second vowel in a variation of the old favorite, "When two vowels go walking, the first one does the talking."

Teaching Tips

✓ The final "e" acts as a signal to make the vowel before it long, but only if one letter separates the vowel and the final "e."

✓ Watch out for words ending with a *v* sound, such as *have*, *glove*, and *love*; they are likely to be "rule breakers."

AT THE KITCHEN TABLE

WHEN TWO VOWELS GO WALKING . . .

Say each of these words out loud. Think about the sound that the vowel makes. Check with your parent to be sure you are saying each sound correctly.

cut	stove	strap	twist
twice	quit	flute	flat
split	plane	write	here
phone	slice	muck	frog

Now write each word in the column where it belongs. If the word contains a short vowel sound, write it in the first column. If the word contains a long vowel sound, write it in the second column. Ask your parent to check your work to be sure you have each word in the correct column.

Short Vowel Sounds	Long Vowel Sounds

On the Go. . .

SPOT THE MAGIC "E"

While riding in the car, see who can find the most words with a final "e." Look on road signs, bumper stickers, license plates, and billboards. Award one point for each word found with a final "e." Award two points for each rule breaker found. Rule breakers include such words as *glove, have,* and *love.* Your child can keep score by counting on his or her fingers or by keeping a tally on a pad of paper.

On Your Own

WHAT HAPPENED TO THE MAGIC?

Sometimes the magic "e" isn't so full of magic. When the magic doesn't work, we call the word a "rule breaker." Here are some rule breaker words with a final "e" that has lost its magic: *love, glove, dove.* The first vowel does not have a long vowel sound, even though there is a final "e." Make a list of as many of these rule breakers as you can think of. Then write a silly poem using these rule breaker words.

TALL TALES TIME

Write a funny story using at least 10 short vowel words and 10 long vowel words. Challenge yourself and add rule breakers too! The more words you use, the more practice you'll get.

IMAGINE THAT!

The English language is 85 percent phonetic. If you know your phonics, you will be able to sound out almost anything!

SOFT SOUNDS AND HARD SOUNDS

Parents' Corner

The letters "c" and "g" are very difficult for young readers because they each have two different sounds. The letter "c" can have both the sound *k* as in *cat* and the sound *s* as in *city*. The letter "g" can have both the sound *g* as in *great* and the sound *j* as in *giant*. Beginning readers often find it difficult to tell the difference between a "j" and a soft "g" and an "s" and a soft "c" in a spoken word. Practice and repeated experience with words using these two letters will help your child learn to pronounce them correctly.

The best way to teach your child these sound patterns is to teach the "e," "i," or "y" signals. The hard sounds are much more common than the soft sounds.

The "e," "i," and "y" Phonics Rule
If an "e," "i," or "y" comes after the letter "c,"
the letter "c" makes the soft *s* sound as in *city*.
If an "e," "i," or "y" comes after the letter "g,"
the letter "g" makes the soft *j* sound as in *giant*.

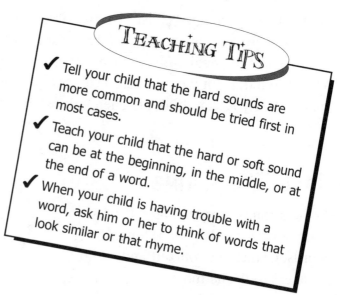

TEACHING TIPS

✔ Tell your child that the hard sounds are more common and should be tried first in most cases.

✔ Teach your child that the hard or soft sound can be at the beginning, in the middle, or at the end of a word.

✔ When your child is having trouble with a word, ask him or her to think of words that look similar or that rhyme.

AT THE KITCHEN TABLE

SOFT OR HARD, LET'S FIND THEM ALL!

Look through the newspaper or a magazine for words containing the letters "c" and "g." Write each word you find in the correct column below. Remember that the hard or soft sound can be at the beginning, in the middle, or at the end of a word. Say each word out loud before you write it down. Ask your parent to find any words you may have missed. Add these words to your list, too. Then say each word out loud to show your parent that you have each word in the correct column. Here are some examples to get you started.

Soft "g" (j)	Soft "c" (s)	Hard "g" (g)	Hard "c" (k)
gem	city	stag	cat

On the Go. . .

CAN YOU TELL ME HOW TO SPELL?

Say three words that have the *j* sound. Challenge your child to tell you which words have the letter "g" and which words have the letter "j." Do the same thing with the letter "c" and the letter "s." Some words won't have either sound. Here are a few to get you started: *giant, gem, jam; small, sat, city; cent, sale, sidewalk; circus, stage, ice; just, jingle, giraffe; judge, magic, page; face, stuck, mice; rice, lass, fence.*

On Your Own

ON YOUR MARK, GET SET, GO!

Just for Fun!

When does the cart come before the horse?
In the dictionary!

Get a clean piece of paper and borrow the kitchen timer. See how many words with a soft *g* sound you can write down in three minutes. Now get ready to time yourself on soft *c* words. Then list all the hard *g* words you can think of in three minutes. Finally list hard *c* words. What was your highest score? Try it again to see if you can beat your first score with more practice.

SIGHT WORDS AND CHECK-UP

Set Your Sights on These Sight Words

the	of	hour	was	what	there
their	said	do	many	some	love
would	two	could	been	world	word
heart	great	who	people	through	though
work	although	tough	water	fold	give
against	thought	both	should	brief	always
young	once	whole	sign	told	mother

Back-to-Basics Check-Up

Have your child read the following words aloud. Put a check by any word he or she has trouble reading.

fad	less	clop	great	gust
skill	stack	globe	whole	blend
crept	till	stuff	male	plume
female	would	smog	gift	grin
tank	jig	space	cage	crisp
slag	face	smite	skid	yell
scale	price	flop	grip	mix
pole	give	scads	pod	hunt

Ask your child to fill in the first column of the table on the next page with the words that he or she found difficult to read. Then work with your child to place a check in any of the remaining columns that describe the word. When the table is completed, you will be able to see which rules or activities your child needs to practice some more. To be sure your child gets the necessary practice, put these difficult words on flash cards and shuffle them in with the sight words for more review.

Word	Short Vowel	Final "e"	Consonant Pair	Soft "c"/"g"	Hard "c"/"g"	Sight Word

Chapter 2

Learning the Vowel Plus "r" Rules

THE ROOSTER'S CROW

Parents' Corner

Not all vowel sounds are as consistent as the short vowels discussed and practiced in chapter 1. Some vowel sounds change when they are influenced by other letters. This is especially true with the letter "r;" this consonant changes the sound of the vowel that it immediately follows. In this lesson, your child will learn to quickly recognize the most common sounds of vowels plus "r." (Reading specialists call these "r"-controlled vowels.) Other letters, such as "l" and "w," may also change the sound of the vowel that precedes them (*all, saw*), but these sound changes are not as consistent as those for the "r"-controlled vowels.

When the letter "r" is found in a word just after an "e," "i," or "u," the "r" causes the vowel to take on a sound that is neither long nor short. The rooster's crow of "er, er, er" is similar to the sound these letter combinations make. The *er* sound heard at the end of a word is usually spelled "er." The *er* sound heard in the middle of a word is usually spelled "ir" or "ur." Help your child recognize and distinguish the sounds created by these two-letter combinations when they appear in words. Review the "er," "ir," "ur" rule:

TEACHING TIPS

✓ Teach your child that "r," "l," and "w" often change the sounds of "e," "i," and "o" in the same syllables.

✓ Remind your child that "er," "ir," and "ur" all sound like *er*, even though they don't look the same.

✓ Point out that "er" usually comes at the end of a word, whereas "ir" and "ur" are often in the middle of the word.

The "er," "ir," "ur" Rule
When the letter "r" comes after an "e," "i," or "u,"
the two letters work together to make the *er* sound.

AT THE KITCHEN TABLE

MIX AND MATCH

Read the clues. Write "ir," "er," or "ur" in the blanks to make a word that answers the clue. Then write the word that you made on the line provided. Now ask your parent to check your answers as you read them out loud. Were all your matches good ones?

1. an animal with feathers   b __ __ d   _____

2. a green plant   f __ __ n   _____

3. mail from a friend   lett __ __   _____

4. a camping light   lant __ __ n   _____

5. the edge of a sidewalk   c __ __ b   _____

6. something you wear   sh __ __ t   _____

7. what fire does   b __ __ n   _____

8. another word for mix   st __ __   _____

9. to be in pain   h __ __ t   _____

10. to spin   wh __ __ l   _____

11. soil or sand   d __ __ t   _____

12. a kind of heater   f __ __ nace   _____

13. a female child   g __ __ l   _____

14. a group of cows   h __ __ d   _____

15. a flowery smell   p __ __ fume   _____

16. the sound a cat makes   p __ __ r   _____

17. an animal with a hard shell   t __ __ tle   _____

18. a shoe without laces   loaf __ __   _____

19. something round   c __ __ cle   _____

20. to act out a play   p __ __ form   _____

On Your Own

CREATE A COMIC STRIP

On a clean sheet of paper make three columns with the following as column heads

"er" Words   "ir" Words   "ur" Words

Now pick a favorite story or book and look for all the "er," "ir," and "ur" words. If you've picked a long book, list only the words from the first three pages. Write the words in the correct columns as you find them. Do any of your words belong in more than one column? If so, be sure to copy the word twice. Now, using the characters from your favorite story or book, create a comic strip story using as many of the vowel plus "r" words on your list as you can. Illustrate your comic strips with funny pictures!

On the Go. . .

FOLLOW THE LEADER

Repeated exposure to words containing the *er* sound is the best way to practice this concept. One fun way to get extra practice is to play Follow the Leader. Challenge your child to say *er* words in a special order. Begin with the first consonant in the alphabet, and take turns with your child saying *er* words that begin with the next consonant letter of the alphabet. Here's an example:

Parent: burn
Child: clerk
Parent: dirt
Child: fern

If this is too easy, try playing it using only one spelling of the *er* sound.

WHEN IS A DOOR NOT A DOOR? WHEN IT'S AJAR

Parents' Corner

The previous lesson discussed what happens to the sounds of "e," "i," and "u" when they are followed by the letter "r." The vowel sounds of the letters "a" and "o" are also changed when they are followed by the letter "r." The "a" plus "r" combination usually makes the *ar* sound, as in *card* and *sharp*. The "o" plus "r" combination usually makes the *or* sound, as in *ford* and *short*. The words with the *or* sound and the *ar* sound are easier to tell apart than "er," "ir," "ur" words because they make very different sounds. Review the "ar" and "or" rule and memory poem with your child:

The "ar" and "or" Rule
When "a" is followed by "r," the two letters work together to make the sound *ar*.
When "o" is followed by "r," the two letters work together to make the sound *or*.

Memory Poem
"a" plus "r" says *ar,* as in "Mark parked dark cars."
"o" plus "r" says *or,* as in "Mort stored worn Fords."

This concept relates to spelling as well as to reading and has two learning objectives. The first objective is to learn the sounds made by the different vowel plus "r" letter combinations. The second and equally important objective is to recognize and distinguish the sounds created by these two-letter combinations when they appear in words.

AT THE KITCHEN TABLE

ARE YOU CLUED IN?

Find the word in this list that matches each clue. Write the word on the line next to the clue and circle the vowel plus "r" letters in the word you have written. Now ask your parent to check your work. Were you clued in?

IMAGINE THAT!
No words rhyme with *orange*, *silver*, or *purple*.

short	sharp	sports	
bark	orange	thorn	
barn	corn	pork	far
hard	car	forest	shark

1. the name for meat from a pig   _____

2. something yellow that you eat   _____

3. an animal that lives in the water   _____

4. watch out for this part of a plant   _____

5. something that you can park   _____

6. the opposite of tall   _____

7. the outside of a tree   _____

8. baseball and football   _____

9. a place where farm animals live   _____

10. not soft   _____

11. a place where wild animals live   _____

12. a knife is   _____

13. a kind of fruit   _____

14. a long way from here   _____

On Your Own

HARD-TO-FIND WORDS THAT RHYME

Circle all the words in an old newspaper or magazine with vowel plus "r" letter combinations. To make it more fun, circle the "er" sound combinations in red, the "ar" vowel combinations in blue, and the "or" vowel combinations in green. On a clean sheet of paper, make three columns labeled "er," "or," and "ar" and write down all the words you found. Choose words from one column and write a rhyming story with them. It's easy to rhyme when you have a word list like this, isn't it? Can you make a rhyme using words from the two remaining columns? Is your rhyme silly or serious? Which kind of rhyme is easier to write?

On the Go. . .

SAY IT AND SPELL IT

Here's a fast and fun word game that will help your child develop reading skills by identifying vowel plus "r" sounds and spellings in words. Say a word that has at least one "ar" or "or" letter combination, such as *car*. Have your child quickly call out the "ar" or "or" letters that he or she thinks are in the word. Your child scores one point each time he or she spells the sound correctly. You score one point for each incorrect spelling. Players keep score on their fingers. The first player to score ten points wins, and the game starts again.

SIGHT WORDS AND CHECK-UP

Set Your Sights on These Sight Words

a	to	you	are	from
have	one	were	your	other
into	only	find	very	where
most	another	put	again	come
does	old	often	want	school
something	enough	four	head	above
friend	kind	sometimes	almost	walk

Vowel Plus "r" Check-Up

Learning all five vowel plus "r" combinations takes time and practice. Have your child write "ar," "er," "ir," "ur," or "or" to complete each word in the story. Make flashcards of any words your child has trouble spelling. Use them to sharpen your child's skill with the vowel plus "r" combinations. Have your child use the following word list for help, or challenge your child to figure out the words without looking at the list.

store	dangerous	mark	Harvey
were	her	sorting	worry
father	darted	smirked	better
blurted	Shirley	sharp	grocery
porch	forks	hurt	storage
arm	corks		

One day (1) Sh__ __ley and (2) h__ __ friend (3) H__ __vey (4) w__ __e sitting on

the (5) p__ __ch. They (6) w__ __re (7) s__ __ting through some old (8) st__ __age

boxes. They found a box of (9) c__ __ks, a box of (10) f___ks, and a box of

(11) sh__ __p knives. (12) Sh__ __ley said, (13) "Sh__ __p knives are

(14) dang__ __ous. We should tell my (15) fath__ __." (16) Aft__ __ (17) Sh__ __ley

went to get (18) h__ __ (19) fath__ __, (20) H__ __vey decided to (21) m__ __k the

box of (22) sh__ __p knives. He wrote on one, then (23) st__ __ted to (24) m__ __k

(25) anoth__ __ box, but he (26) h__ __t his (27) __ __m on the (28) sh__ __p

knives. (29) Fath__ __ (30) d__ __ted to (31) H__ __vey's side. (32) H__ __vey

(33) bl__ __ted, "Ow! I (34) h__ __t my (35) __ __m!" Luckily, (36) Fath__ __ was

a (37) n__ __se. (38) Fath__ __ cleaned (39) H__ __vey's (40) __ __m and told him

not to (41) w__ __ry. (42) Fath__ __ (43) sm__ __ked and said, "All (44) bett__ __.

Then, (45) Fath__ __, (46) H__ __vey, and (47) Sh__ __ley went to the

(48) groc__ __y (49) st__ __e to buy some ice cream.

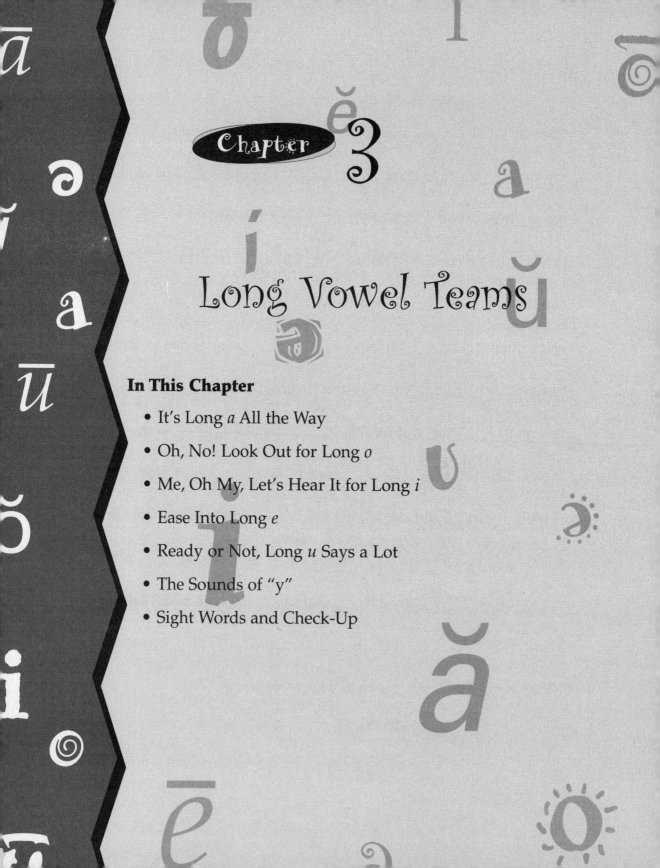

Chapter 3

Long Vowel Teams

In This Chapter

- It's Long *a* All the Way
- Oh, No! Look Out for Long *o*
- Me, Oh My, Let's Hear It for Long *i*
- Ease Into Long *e*
- Ready or Not, Long *u* Says a Lot
- The Sounds of "y"
- Sight Words and Check-Up

IT'S LONG A ALL THE WAY

Parents' Corner

There are only five long vowel sounds, but each sound has several spellings. Your child will need a great deal of practice before instantly recognizing and reading these long vowel sounds and accurately spelling the words containing them. The single long vowel spellings of "a," "e," "i," "o," and "u" each represent the long vowel sounds when at the end of syllables and are discussed in detail in chapter 6. This chapter focuses on the most common vowel team spellings of each long vowel sound. The vowel team spellings have two letters that represent one long vowel sound. With practice, your child will be able to quickly recognize and correctly pronounce each of these vowel team spellings.

The Magic "e" activities in chapter 1 show one way to spell words that have a long *a* sound. But two other vowel team spellings for this sound also occur frequently. They are "ai" as in *rain* and "ay" as in *day*. One additional spelling is not seen quite as often, but is useful to learn. That is "eigh" as in *sleigh*. Review the long *a* sound with your child, and ask your child to think of as many words as possible that have the long *a* sound.

Teaching Tips

✓ A long *a* sound says its own name.

✓ Unlike the short a sound, the long a sound has many different spellings.

✓ The four most common spellings of the long a sound are "ai" as in *rain*, "ay" as in *day*, "a_e" as in *cake*, "eigh" as in *eight*.

✓ Remind your child to use his or her knowledge of word groups or families to figure out new long a sound words.

AT THE KITCHEN TABLE

LET'S SET SAIL IN THE BAY

Two ways to spell words with a long a sound are by using the letters "ai" and "ay." The following words use these two spellings. Use this list of words to complete the fill-in-the-blank sentences. Then place the words in the crossword puzzle on page 37. When you've finished, read the completed sentences out loud to your parent.

bay   sail   stain   clay   pay   stay   snail   bait   maid   rain

Across

3. The ship's _____ filled when the wind blew.

4. My dad likes to use worms as _____ when he goes fishing.

5. My brother said he would _____ for us to go to the movies.

6. We have a new _____ in our fish tank.

7. The flowers need the _____ to grow.

Down

1. My mom would like a _____ to help her around the house.

2. My sister, Lora, ordered a large _____ pot for her plant.

3. I have a _____ on my baseball uniform from sliding on the grass.

4. The whales swam into the _____.

6. My dog likes to _____ in his doghouse when it rains.

LET'S TAKE A SLEIGH TODAY

You can also spell words with a long a sound using "eigh" or by following the Magic "e" rule. You can complete the sleigh crossword puzzle if you follow these clues. Place the correct word from this list in the space next to each clue. Ask your parent to check your answers.

snake	lake
eight	chase
cage	weight
sleigh	bake

Across

3. the number after seven _____

4. something you ride through the snow on _____

5. a place where you can keep a pet hamster _____

7. something dogs like to do to cats _____

Down

1. a place to go fishing _____

2. something a scale measures _____

4. a long animal that slithers _____

6. a way to cook in an oven _____

Did you slip up along the way? Now fill in the crossword puzzle!

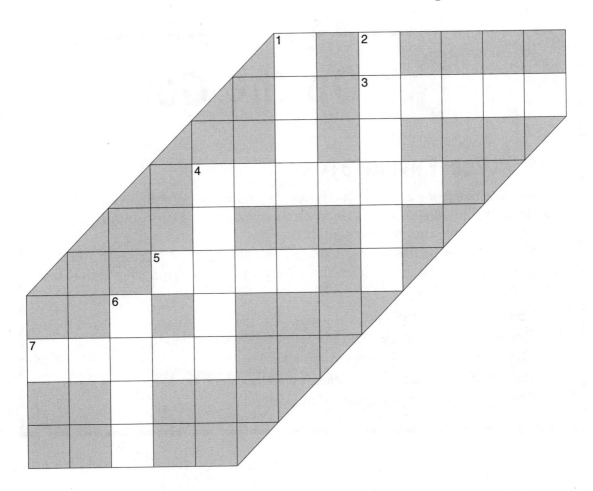

On Your Own

ONE RHYME AT A TIME

Write a story or poem using as many long *a* words as you can. Here is a sample of a silly long *a* poem:

There once was a lady from Spain.
She claimed to find snakes in the rain.
She drank lemonade,
While all day she swayed,
On a swing, by the lake, in the shade.

On the Go...

THE NEVER-ENDING STORY

You can play this game any time you have a few minutes—or much longer. Here's how to start. Say a sentence that ends with a word with a long *a* sound. Now ask your child to make up the next sentence in the story, again being sure the last word in the sentence has a long *a* sound. The story can be as silly or weird or funny as you can make it, but keep those long *a* words coming. Here is how one story began:

Today I played in the rain.
But nobody got wet because the rain was made of paper.
Then Sally said, "Let's jump in the lake."
But when we jumped in the lake, it was too much to take.
The paper lake broke from all of our weight!

OH, NO! LOOK OUT FOR LONG O

Parents' Corner

Many long vowel sounds are spelled with two vowels together. Just as with consonant teams that consist of two letters with one consonant sound (see chapter 1), these vowel teams have one long vowel sound. There are three common vowel team spellings for the long *o* sound. They are "ow" as in *snow*, "oa" as in *boat*, and "o_e" as in *slope*.

When your child is studying phonics, remind him or her to build on prior knowledge. Your child already knows the "o_e" spelling pattern from the Magic "e" exercises in chapter 1. Your child also learns by analogy, and intermediate-age children have a large supply of words they have already learned. Help your child draw from these words to compare sounds and spellings.

With the long *o* sound, it is especially helpful to teach the "old" and "ost" word family patterns. Explain to your child that the letters "old" almost always say *old*, and the letters "ost" almost always say *ost*, as in *most*. It is equally important to describe to your child the exceptions to the rules. For example, there are two different sounds for the "ow" spelling. One of the sounds is the long *o*. The other sound is heard at the beginning of *owl* and at the end of *how*. Readers are often confused by the "ow" spelling of the long *o* sound because "ow" has a very different sound in many common words that your child probably already knows, such as *now*, *cow*, *how*, and *owl*.

TEACHING TIPS

✓ A long *o* sound says its own name.

✓ Unlike the short *o* sound, the long *o* sound has many different spellings.

✓ Introduce the three commons spellings of the long *o* sound: "ow" as in *snow*, "oa" as in *boat*, and "o_e" as in *choke*.

AT THE KITCHEN TABLE

DO YOU KNOW HOW TO GLOAT?

Write a story using as many "ow" and "oa" words as you can. Use words such as *blow* and *goat*. When you have finished, make a copy of the story, but leave out the "ow" and "oa" words. Put a line for someone to write on in place of each "ow" and "oa" word that you remove. Give the story to your parent to read. Can your parent figure out what words you left out? If you can stump your mom or dad, you get to gloat!

On Your Own

SPILL AND SPELL

Here is a jumble of perfectly good long *o* words. Pick the ones from this list that complete the sentences best. Did you find one word for each blank? Good!

toast	mow	soak	show	blown
groan	town	roast	short	row
boat	pillow	slope	floats	mope
hope	goat	coach	coats	crow
plows	glow	sown	load	grown

1. Before washing my shirt, I will _____ it in cold water.

2. The ship had _____ off course during to the storm.

3. The old _____ was chewing on a tin can.

4. I like to _____ marshmallows when we go camping.

5. Last weekend we took our

   _____ and went

   fishing in the lake.

6. If you don't win, don't sit around and _____.

7. I _____ our school wins the spelling bee.

8. Mr. Smith is the new _____ of the football team.

9. The snow _____ will be clearing the streets soon.

10. The boy was happy to _____ his mother his report card.

11. The trees had _____ very tall.

12. Lee saw a _____ flying across the sky.

13. When you make your bed, don't forget the

_____ cases.

14. We admired all the pretty

_____ in the parade.

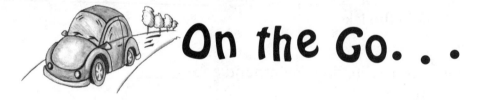

On the Go. . .

GROCERIES GALORE!

Many items at the grocery store have long *o* vowel sounds. When you and your child are shopping, start reading the names of the products and brands that have a long *o* sound (e.g., Crisco, Tostitos, Nabisco). See who is first to find ten items with this sound. To challenge your child further, agree to count only those items with one of the three long *o* spellings: "ow," "oa," or "o_e." Happy hunting.

WHO TOLD THE MOST?

Challenge your child to an "old" and "ost" word family pattern contest. Next time you're riding in the car, alternate saying words that have the "old" sound—such as *gold, hold, mold*—until one of you is stumped. Then switch to "ost" sounds. Don't forget to use multi-syllabic words.

ME, OH MY, LET'S HEAR IT FOR LONG I

Parents' Corner

The long *i* sound has four different vowel team spellings and several exceptions. Three of these spellings are covered in this lesson: "i_e" as in *mile*, "igh" as in *high*, and "ie" as in *tie*. The long *i* sound is also spelled as a "y" at the end of syllables, but this will be covered later in the chapter.

Of the four long *i* vowel team spellings, the "ie" spelling can be the trickiest. Sometimes it sounds like a long *i* (as in *pie*), but sometimes it sounds like a long *e* (as in *piece*). In the case of "ie," it does not help much to sort words by the spelling pattern, but it is important for your child to practice reading words with both sounds. Repeated reading and spelling practice with these "ie" spellings will help your child be able to automatically recognize the correct pronunciations. Learning different pronunciations for the same spellings will help your child become a more flexible reader and speller.

TEACHING TIPS

✓ Teach your child the "igh," as in *high*, and "ie," as in *tie*, long *i* spellings.

✓ Review the "i_e" spelling introduced in chapter 1.

✓ Explain to your child that the "ie" spelling is tricky. Sometimes it sounds like a long *i* and sometimes it sounds like a long *e*.

Just as with the other long vowels, the long *i* sound can be compared with the same long *i* spellings in other words. If students are able to rhyme well, they can recognize sound spellings by analogy. Helping your child to rhyme is important to his or her reading and spelling development. Remind your child that rhymes can occur in any part of the word, not just at the ends of syllables.

AT THE KiTCHEN TABLE

GiVE ME A HiGH FiVE

The vowel pair "ie" can be tricky. Sometimes it stands for the long *i* sound, and sometimes it stands for the long *e* sound. Sort this list of words into the Long *i* Sound "ie" Spelling and the Long *e* Sound "ie" Spelling columns. When you have finished sorting the words, say all the words in each column out loud with your parent to check your choices. If you got them all right, celebrate with a high five with your parent.

thief	dried	niece	duties
pie	grief	believe	tried
supplies	untie	flies	stories
skies	cities	dies	berries
chief	pieces	cherries	fries

Long *i* Sound "ie" Spellings	**Long *e* Sound "ie" Spellings**

On Your Own

CAN YOU TELL THIS STORY?

In this story, the "i_e," "igh," and "ie" have been left out of the words. Can you make sense of this nonsense? Write the correct missing letters in the blanks to complete the story.

On a dark (1) n__ __ __t a long time ago, a brave (2) kn__ __ __t was

sitting (3) h__ __ __ upon his horse. Suddenly, he saw a (4) l__ __ __t. It

gave him a (5) fr__ __ __t, but he was ready to (6) f__ __ __t. He picked

up his (7) sh__ __ld and started to (8) r__d__ his horse toward the

(9) l__ __ __t. After a (10) f__v__-minute (11) r__d__ he reached the

(12) l_____t. It was (13) qu__t__ a (14) rel__ __f for the (15) kn__ __ __t to

find the (16) l__ __ __t was the camp (17) f__r__ of a friend.

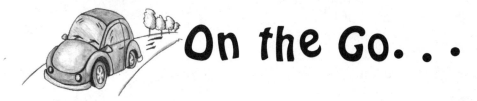

On the Go. . .

THE LONG VOWEL WALK

Take a long vowel walk with your child to practice the long *i* vowel sound. Look for things with the long *i* vowel sound. See who can find the most things with names that contain the sound. For example, on the playground there are climbing poles and the high slide. During a walk through your neighborhood you might see someone with a smile or the sidewalk that you walk on. Be creative! There are lots of long *i* sounds all around.

EASE INTO LONG E

Parents' Corner

The long *e* sound and its spellings are the easiest of the long vowels to learn. This is because there are only two common vowel team spellings for the long *e* sound, the "ee" as in *street* and the "ea" as in *mean*. The final "e" spelling, as in *compete*, introduced in chapter 1, is not a common spelling; indeed, words with a final "e" that have a long *e* sound are quite rare. Chapter 6 will discuss the long *e* "e" spelling at the end of a syllable. The final "y" at the end of a word can also have the long *e* sound, but this will be covered later in this chapter.

There are some infrequent variations of the long *e* spellings. In the "i" before "e" spelling rule, for example, "ei" following a "c" can have the long *e* sound:

The "i" Before "e" Memory Poem
"i" before "e", like *believe*,
Except after "c", like *receive*,
Or sounding like $\bar{a}$ as in *neighbor* or *sleigh*,
Where "e" before "i" is the way.

The "ea" spelling is usually pronounced as a long *e*, but there are exceptions to the "When two vowels go walking, the first one does the talking" rule. The "ea" spelling can have the short *e* sound as in *bread* or even the long *a* sound as in *great*. Although memorizing phonics and spelling rules is very worthwhile, it is also important for your child to learn to be flexible.

> **TEACHING TIPS**
>
> ✔ Remind your child that two vowels together often stand for one vowel sound, such as "ee" in *street* and "ea" as in *mean*.
>
> ✔ Explain that there are a few exceptions to the "ea" long e sound. Sometimes "ea" makes the short e sound, as in *bread*, and sometimes the long a sound, as in *great*.

AT THE KITCHEN TABLE

THE UNWANTED VISITOR

The letters "ee" and "ea" work together to make the long *e* sound. Read this story about a most unusual visitor. Then, on a separate sheet of paper, write all of the "ee" and "ea" words that have a long *e* sound.

Once upon a time, a mean, green beast lived near a small farming village. The farmers living in the village lived in constant fear. The beast would sneak onto their farms, tear up their gardens, and eat what it liked. When the beast was thirsty, it would break into a barn and steal the farmers' cream. When the beast was hungry, it would feast on the farmer's sheep, grazing down by the creek.

The farmers had a meeting to see what they could do to catch the beast. They worked as a team to weave a strong net, and they hung the net between two trees by the creek where the net could not easily be seen. The very next day, the beast wandered down to the creek for a bath and got caught in the net. Three of the strongest farmers carried the beast deep into the forest to live far away from their village. The beast was happy living in the forest, and the farmers of the small village lived happily ever after.

Do you have thirty-one words on your list? If so, you found them all. Now let's have some fun. Instead of the ending shown here, create your own ending to this story. Use lots of long *e* sound words. Read this new story to your parent. Which ending has the most long *e* sound words?

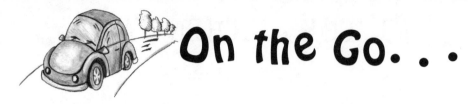

On the Go...

THE CHANGE GAME

Words with a long *e* sound are quite common, and many other words can be changed into new words by replacing the vowel with a long *e* vowel sound. You can help your child practice this by playing the Change Game. Say a word without the long *e* sound and ask your child to change the vowel to the long *e* sound and say the new word. For example, when you say *bat*, your child says, *beat*. Score one point for each word changed. When your child gets ten points, switch roles and have your child think of the words. As a challenge, have your child tell you how the spelling changes when the vowel sound changes. In the example above, the "a" changes to "ea" for the long *e* vowel sound.

On Your Own

SPECTACULAR SPELLING EXCEPTIONS

The vowel team "ea" doesn't always make the long *e* sound. Sometimes "ea" makes the short *e* sound, as in *bread*. Once in a while, it makes the long *a* sound, as in *great*.

Divide a piece of notebook paper into three columns. Label the first column Long *e* "ea" Words. Label the second column Short *e* "ea" Words. Label the third column Long *a* "ea" Words. Get an old newspaper or magazine, and start looking for "ea" words. Find as many words as you can for each column. When you have finished making your lists, practice reading aloud the words you found. If you practice this often, you can become a spectacular speller too!

Just for Fun!
What starts with E, ends with E, and only has one letter? An envelope.

READY OR NOT, LONG U SAYS A LOT!

Parents' Corner

The letter "u" represents more sounds than any other letter of the alphabet. The short *u* sound can be spelled in many different ways. Sometimes it gets a little confusing!

The long *u* vowel sound is made by speaking the letter name. At the end of a syllable, the "u" makes the long *u* sound (see chapter 6), as in *super*. With the vowel team spellings, the long *u* sound can be pronounced in two ways:

- The "ew" spelling can have the long *u* sound, as in *few* and *view*. However, there are very few long *u* words with this spelling. The "ew" spelling can also represent the *oo* sound, as in *knew* and *flew*.
- The Magic "e" rule says that the "u_e" spelling should have the long *u* vowel sound. This works with such words as *cute* and *mule*. However, there are exceptions. In *tube*, *dude*, and *June*, the final "e" signals the "u" to make the *oo* sound, as in *zoo*. See chapter 4 for more spelling examples of this *oo* vowel sound.

TEACHING TIPS

✓ Introduce the long *u* vowel team spellings of "u_e" as in *mule* and *dude* and "ew" as in *few* and *view*.

✓ Teach your child to hear the difference between the long *u* sound and the *oo* sound in words.

Introduce the long *u* sound to your child. Remind your child that it is the sound that is made when the letter name is spoken. Tell your child that sometimes a word with the same spelling pattern looks as if it has the long *u* sound, but it sounds a little different—like the *oo* sound in *zoo*. Be careful to correct any *oo* sounds when you practice the long *u*. This will help with proper pronunciation and spelling.

AT THE KITCHEN TABLE

WANT ADS

Find an old newspaper and look for the classified advertisements section. As you read through the ads, circle the long *u* sound words that you find. Then read the ads out loud to your parent. This will help you hear the sounds better. Watch out for tricky *oo* sounds. Here are some sample ads. Can you find all the long *u* sound words?

Pets 4 Sale

Four cute Standard Poodle puppies must be sold soon. These dogs grow to be huge and are usually excellent human companions. Call Sue or Hugh for details at 875-4543.

Old Record Sale

Tired of that new music? Want to press the mute button whenever your daughter turns on the stereo? Few songs today are as good as they used to be. Just call old Ice Cube for super titles and prices at 765-9843.

On the Go. . .

SCAVENGER HUNT

While you do the dishes or clean the house with your child, think of long *u* sound items that you could find in every room of your home. Take turns naming off items. Perhaps start with the *vacuum* in the coat closet and go from there. You can also play this game while driving down the road or waiting for an appointment. Simply name a place, such as the grocery store, and try to come up with as many long *u* sound items as you can.

On Your Own

RESEARCH "U"

Find a large container. For one week, use it to collect the "junk mail," advertisements, catalogs, flyers, and product pamphlets that companies send to your home. Read through it all and use a highlighter or marking pen to mark words that have the long *u* sounds. Write all the words you find on a list, and tack it up on the wall by your bed. Practice reading these words every night before you go to sleep. In less than a week you will be able to speed-read all the words you have found. Then you can graduate from "U" University!

THE SOUNDS OF "Y"

Parents' Corner

The two long vowel sounds of "y" are fun to teach and relatively easy for young readers to learn. This is because there are two rules, both easy to remember and easy to use, that let the reader know what sound the letter "y" is going to make. Of course, just to keep things tricky, the "y" also has a consonant sound as in *yellow* and *beyond*.

When the letter "y" is at the end of a word that contains a vowel and a consonant, the "y" makes the long *e* sound, as in *baby* and *happy*. When the letter "y" is at the end of word that does not have a vowel and a consonant, the "y" makes a long *i* sound as in *my* and *crying*. A "y" at the end of a long word, such as *merrily*, says long *e*, but a "y" at the end of a short word, such as *try*, says long *i*. Remember, short words, such as *try* and *cry*, can add endings such as "-ing," but the "y" spelling still keeps the long *i* sound.

Adding endings to words ending in "y" presents some spelling difficulties. Prima's *Better Spelling in 5 Minutes a Day* gives The Final "y" Rule, which should help:

The Final "y" Rule

If a word ends in a vowel and then a "y," keep the "y" and add the ending (*play/played*). If a word ends in a consonant and then a "y," change the "y" to "i" and add the ending (*beauty/beautiful*), but keep the "y" if the ending begins with an "i" (*baby/babyish*).

AT THE KITCHEN TABLE

THE LONG AND SHORT OF "Y"

Read the following list of words. Pay special attention to the sound the "y" makes in each word. Write the words that have the long *e* sound under the Long *e* column. Write the words that have the long *i* sound under the Long *i* column.

many	why	sticky	cry	pretty	snowy
sunny	my	healthy	by	carry	fly
nightly	pry	sky	soapy	dry	shy
turkey	celery	spy	easy	try	sly

Long *e* as in *happy*	**Long *i* as in *my***

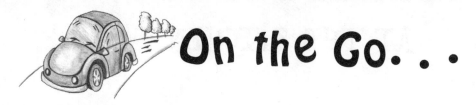

On the Go. . .

I Spy The Letter "y"

Find an object that is spelled with a final "y," such as a fly, and then say, "I spy the letter 'y'." Your child then asks, "Does it sound like long *e* or long *i*?" You have to say whether the letter "y" makes the long *e* or long *i* sound. In this case, you would say, "It sounds like long *i*." Then your child must find and name the object. Take turns calling out, "I spy the letter 'y'."

On Your Own

An Adjective Adventure

Many of words that end in the letter "y" are used to describe things. We call these words adjectives. Adjectives tell us something more about the thing we are describing. For example, a muddy boot tells us something about that boot—it's too dirty to wear into the house! See how many adjectives you can think of that end in the letter "y." Write them down on a piece of paper. If you're not sure about the spelling, check in a dictionary. After you have a long list of adjectives ending in the letter

"y," write a story using as many words from the list as you can. See if you can write a funny, scary, or silly story.

SIGHT WORDS AND CHECK-UP

Set Your Sights on These Sight Words

earth	wild	country	weather	father
watch	someone	eyes	field	gold
today	everyone	build	sure	picture
heard	warm	brought	answer	mind
true	learn	early	instead	blue
toward	piece	built	hold	talk
front	cold	done	money	tough

Other Vowel Sounds Check-Up

Many children have a hard time learning the many spellings for the long vowel sounds. You may need to review some earlier activities if you find that your child has trouble with words in this review. It is a good idea to put the spellings for each of the long vowel sounds on a 3×5 card for reference. Allow your child to use the cards as often as needed as you work through the review activities.

Read the first word in each row aloud. Then read the three word choices. Have your child tell you which word has the same vowel sound as the first word in each row.

1. **mate**	mall	bait	can
2. **goats**	fled	gorilla	snow
3. **spread**	grand	melt	scale
4. **claimed**	bring	blame	stamp
5. **leave**	stripe	greed	scale
6. **bruised**	flow	strapped	choose
7. **paints**	rice	treats	way
8. **pew**	pets	view	wept

9. **poach**	sport	know	champ
10. **squeeze**	chief	chef	chin
11. **sight**	five	peel	both
12. **stow**	brown	loan	short
13. **stray**	strike	sleep	plain
14. **mule**	taunt	dud	use
15. **great**	screen	seal	date

Have your child read the list of words, then read the clues. Your child should then write the word in the blank that matches the clue.

clean	white	high	nice
fright	sly	sweet	thief
few	light	day	huge

16. the same meaning as incredibly large _____

17. the opposite of dirty _____

18. the opposite of night _____

19. the same meaning as kind _____

20. the opposite of black _____

21. the same meaning as fear _____

22. the opposite of low _____

23. the same meaning as clever _____

24. the opposite of dark _____

25. the same meaning as burglar _____

26. the opposite of many _____

27. the same meaning as sugary _____

Vowel Teams and Other Vowel Sounds

In This Chapter

SOUNDS TO ENJOY

Parents' Corner

In chapter 3, your child practiced reading words with two vowels that worked together as vowel teams to make long vowel sounds. In some words, vowel teams work together to stand for vowel sounds that are neither long nor short. We call these sounds "other vowel sounds." As is frequently the case in the English spelling system, the same sound can be spelled in different ways. Fortunately, some of these spellings have rules that work the majority of the time. Prima's *Better Spelling in 5 Minutes a Day* is the companion work to this book and provides easy-to-remember spelling rules to assist the developing young speller.

Two different spellings represent the *oy* sound in words: "oi" and "oy." A simple spelling rule will help your child know which to use as he or she practices reading these spellings: The *oy* sound is usually spelled "oy" if it's at the end of a syllable (*joyful*); other-wise, it's spelled "oi" (*rejoice*).

Perhaps this memory jingle will help your child remember this "oy" vs. "oi" rule:

TEACHING TIPS

✔ Teach your child to correctly pronounce oy as two distinct sounds, opening, then closing the inside of the mouth.

✔ The "oy" spelling is usually found at the end of words, and the "oi" spelling is usually found at the beginning or in the middle of words.

The "oy" vs. "oi" Jingle
End a word part with "o-y"
As in "j-o-y," you see.
Everywhere else, spell "o-i"
As in "j-o-i-n-t."

Your child will need a great deal of practice to read and write words containing these letter patterns with accuracy and confidence.

AT THE KITCHEN TABLE

AHOY TO THE SOUND OF OY

Read each clue. Write an "oi" or "oy" to complete the word that matches each clue. Read the words you have completed out loud to your parent to be sure you are pronouncing it correctly. Then write the whole word on the line next to each clue.

1. to like something   enj__ __ _____

2. what you speak with   v__ __ce _____

3. a male child   b__ __ _____

4. a sound   n__ __se _____

5. nickels, dimes, and quarters   c__ __ns _____

6. balls, games, and dolls   t__ __s _____

7. another name for dirt   s__ __l _____

8. food that turns bad   sp__ __led_____

OH BOY, MORE PRACTICE!

Read each sentence and the words below it. Choose the word that makes sense in each sentence. Write the word in the blank to complete the sentence. Read the complete sentence out loud to your parent. Did you score one hundred percent?

1. Add one half cup of _____ to the cookie mixture.

   soil   oil   joy

2. I like to eat hard-_____ eggs for lunch.

   enjoy   toil   boiled

3. My father _____ the army after high school.

   enjoyed   mouth   joined

4. _____ stayed the same for many years.

   Ploys   Toys   Annoys

5. Small beads are sometimes used in toys to make a rattling

   _____.

   snake   toys   noise

6. I like to have first _____ when we pick a movie to watch.

   plan   enjoy   choice

7. I worked very hard because I did not want to _____ my teacher.

choice disappoint spoil

8. The dockworker used a _____ to lift the large carton.

joist   hoist   boy

9. The temperature of _____ water is 132° Fahrenheit.

cooking   boiling   bouncing

10. It was too _____ to work on my homework.

noisy   oily   special

On Your Own

For Joy! I Spy An Oy!

See how many things you can find in your house that have the "oi" or "oy" spelling. Some good places to look are in the refrigerator, in the cupboards, or in the "junk mail" stack. Keep track of the words you find by writing them on small pieces of paper. When you have finished, sort the papers into two groups: words with "oi" and words with "oy." Practice reading your word cards until you can read them without making any mistakes.

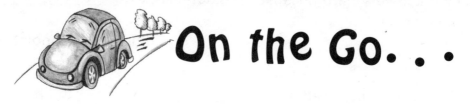

On the Go. . .

SAY THE WORD YOU FEEL

Practice spelling "oi" and "oy" words into your child's palm using your fingers. Take turns doing the spelling. Your child must say each letter as you spell it (and vice versa), and then say the entire word once it is completed. To make this game more challenging, the person whose hand is being spelled into cannot look. If your hand is too ticklish, try spelling the words onto each other's backs. This is also a fun bedtime game.

THE AWESOME SOUND OF "AU" AND "AW"

Parents' Corner

Correct pronunciation is an important key to spelling. When you don't know how to spell a difficult word, you probably sound out the word to hear the individual sounds. Teach your child to use this same spelling strategy when learning "aw" and "au" words.

Introduce the sound of "aw" as in *draw* and "au" as in *caught*. This sound is difficult to spell correctly because there is no spelling rule that can be applied consistently. Only constant exposure in reading text and writing practice can help develop mastery of these "aw" and "au" spellings. Both spellings can start words or be in the middle of words. Only the "aw" spelling can end syllables or words.

To pronounce these words, think about the sound people make when they see a newborn baby or an adorable little puppy. It is a sort of exaggerated short *o* sound. The only difference is that you drop your jaw very low when pronouncing this sound. This is the sound the vowel teams "au" and "aw" represent. Use the following Memory Poem to help your child correctly pronounce this sound.

TEACHING TIPS

✓ Teach your child the correct pronunciation of the *aw* sound.

✓ Show your child the difference between the "aw" spelling, as in *straw* and *draw*, and the "au" spelling, as in *sauce* and *caught*.

✓ Be patient with your child and don't move too quickly to the next activity.

Memory Poem
"a-u" and "a-w"
make the sound of *aaaw*,
To be sure you say it well,
you should drop your jaw.

This sound can change when the "au" and "aw" spellings are combined with the "l," as in *awl* and *haul*.

AT THE KITCHEN TABLE

THE WIZARD OF AAAH'S

Read the list of words below. Then read the sentences that follow. Write the correct word from the list on the blank in each sentence. Then read the completed sentences aloud to your parent to check your answers.

launch	faucet	hawk	crawl	
sauce	caught	straw	laundry	pawn

1. My mom makes the best spaghetti _____ in the world.

2. I saw a red-tailed _____ sitting on a fence post.

3. The hawk _____ a large snake and was going to eat it.

4. My brother lost a _____ from his chess game.

5. Mary's baby sister is learning how to _____.

6. One of my chores at home is to fold the

_____ and put it away.

7. The kitchen _____ has a broken handle.

8. We put _____ in the stalls to keep the calves warm and dry.

9. I watched the _____ of the space shuttle of television.

AW SHUCKS!

Read each clue and fill in the blanks for each word with "au" or "aw." Then write the whole word on the line. Ask your parent to check your work. Are you ten for ten? Good for you!

1. cat and dog feet   p__ __s   _____

2. a young deer   f__ __n   _____

3. to tease   t__ __nt   _____

4. a type of yard   l__ __n   _____

5. your lower face   j__ __   _____

6. a car   __ __to   _____

7. the toe of an eagle   cl__ __   _____

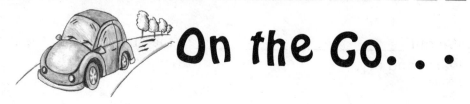

Spot And Check

Take advantage of the minutes you spend in traffic, at the grocery store, or waiting for an appointment by looking for words that have the "au" or "aw" letter combinations in advertisements. When your child spots a word with the "au" or "aw" letter combination, ask your child to read the sentence in which it appears aloud.

On Your Own

An Awfully Big Family

Use the TV guide, the newspaper, a dictionary, old magazines, or whatever printed material you like, and start looking for words with the "aw" and "au" vowel teams. Write the words on small squares of paper, business cards, or some 3 × 5 cards that have been cut in half. Don't stop until you have a huge assortment of "aw" and "au" words. Once you have finished, organize the words you have found by word family (words with the same spelling patterns), and practice reading them out loud. See how fast you can read them all. Then, mix all the words and try reading them again. Can you read them just as quickly even though they are not sorted into work families?

THE TWO SOUNDS OF "OO"

Parents' Corner

As with many of the other vowel sounds, correct pronunciation helps with accurate reading and helps to develop conventional spelling. The letters "oo" stand for two very different sounds in words. The first sound is pronounced for a longer period of time. This is the long *oo* ($\bar{oo}$) sound that is heard in *zoo, moon,* and *spoon.* The second sound represented by the letters "oo" is a short sound. It should be pronounced with a short release of breath. It is almost like the sound you make when you pick up something that is very heavy. This is the short *oo* ($\breve{oo}$) sound that is heard in *hook, cook,* and *book.*

The difficulty with these *oo* sounds is the multitude of spelling options. The long *oo* sound has a wide variety of spellings: "oo" as in *noon,* "ew" as in *dew,* "ui" as in *suit,* "u" as in *super,* and "u_e" as in *clue.* The short *oo* sound is usually spelled "oo" as in *look,* but can also be spelled as "u" as in *butcher.* There are no useful spelling rules to help your child know when to apply the correct spellings for either of these sounds. Only reading and writing practice will help develop conventional spelling of these sounds.

TEACHING TIPS

✓ Teach your child to correctly pronounce the sounds of long *oo* as in *noon* and short *oo* as in *look.*

✓ The long *oo* sound can be spelled with the letters "oo" as in *noon,* "ew" as in *dew,* "ui" as in *suit,* "u" as in *super,* and "u_e" as in *clue.*

✓ The short *oo* sound can be spelled with the letters "oo" as in *look* or a "u" as in *butcher.*

Work carefully when teaching your intermediate-age child these two sounds and their spellings. This lesson deserves particular attention and monitored practice to achieve the results needed to improve reading and spelling.

AT THE KITCHEN TABLE

HUNTING ON THE HOME FRONT

A scavenger hunt is fun, and it is a great way to practice reading also! Play this game with your parents. The object of the game is to see how many items you can find in your house that have either of the two *oo* sounds (long *oo* as in *spoon* or short *oo* as in *book*). Make a list of everything you find. Give yourself and your parent five minutes to find as many "oo" items as possible. When time is up, count up all the items you found. Next time, try playing this game in your yard or at a local park. How many items did you find this time?

"OO" CHALLENGE

Now it's time to work with those pesky *oo* sound words that have spellings other than "oo," such as "ew" as in *dew*, "ui" as in *suit,* "u" as in *super*, "u_e" as in *clue*, and "u" as in *butcher*. Read the following list aloud to your parent. Tell your parent which *oo* sound—long or short—is used in each word.

tutor	suit	sugar	new
fluid	dude	stew	fruit
duty	flute	pushing	juice
tube	duke	crew	cruise
clue	blue	shrew	dew
recruit	pudding	true	pursuit
glue	blew	tune	flew

On Your Own

Look For "Oo" At High Noon

Read the words in the list below. Listen carefully as you read each word aloud. Decide if the word has the long *oo* sound in *noon* or the short *oo* sound in *look*. Then, write the words on the lines under the correct heading.

hood	boot	book	foot
broom	tooth	wood	spoon
hook	shook	moose	nook
food	hoof	stood	took
spool	tools	snoop	goose
gloom	zoom	good	scoot

Long *oo* sound in *noon*	Short *oo* sound in *look*

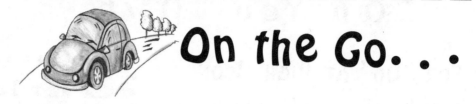

On the Go. . .

LET'S VISIT THE ZOO

The two sounds of "oo" are perfect to use for challenge games when visiting the zoo. As you and your child read about the animals on the zoo signs, look for words that contain the long *oo* sound, as in *spoon*. Have your child call out these words while you count the long *oo* sound words. When you get to ten , start looking for short *oo* sound words, as in *book*. Be sure to count the words with different spellings if the sound your child is choosing is correct.

SIGHT WORDS AND CHECK-UP

Set Your Sights on These Sight Words

move	group	fourth	half	course
ready	hours	carry	either	already
bought	cold	behind	says	heavy
beautiful	become	child	onto	choose
buy	league	court	breath	adventure
ocean	prove	sold	recipe	reign
anger	blind	shove	conquer	ache

"ew," "ui," "oo," and "u_e" Check-Up

Read the first word in each row aloud. Then read the three word choices. Have your child tell you the word that has the same vowel sound as the first word in each row.

1.	**tooth**	below	shone	dune
2.	**suit**	choice	chute	cheat
3.	**hood**	poles	fruit	shook
4.	**blew**	croon	sew	done
5.	**stool**	stood	spoke	brew
6.	**woods**	moat	grown	look
7.	**strewn**	tune	swoop	town
8.	**clue**	logs	spool	smash
9.	**gloom**	coin	blue	toy
10.	**took**	crook	cool	loan
11.	**drew**	pail	three	flue
12.	**hoop**	look	broke	swoon
13.	**brook**	moon	stood	moo
14.	**knew**	suit	float	block
15.	**roof**	stack	stone	cook

"au," "aw," "oi," and "oy" Check-Up

Read the list of words. Then read the clues. Have your child write the correct word on the line next to each clue.

point	boy	sauce	dawn
boiling	enjoyed	loyal	oily
coins	paws	crawl	auto
haul	claws	jaw	launch

1. to begin or send off _____

2. something you can put on pasta _____

3. nickels and dimes _____

4. lower part of your face _____

5. greasy _____

6. to carry something _____

7. another name for a car _____

8. dog and cat feet _____

9. movement using hands and knees _____

10. used by animals for protection _____

11. devoted _____

12. had fun _____

13. bubbling hot _____

14. early morning _____

15. a male child _____

16. the tip of a pencil _____

Chapter 5

Compound Words and Contractions

In This Chapter

- Reading Compound Words
- Understanding Contractions
- Sight Words and Check-Up

READING COMPOUND WORDS

Parents' Corner

After your intermediate-age child has mastered the basics of the sounds and letters that make up our words, he or she needs to move beyond phonics to word study. The activities in this chapter have been developed to introduce your child to the study of word parts and word meanings. The best place to begin this introduction is with compound words. The study of compound words will help your child in two ways. First, your child will learn that words can be broken or divided into smaller parts that are easier to read. Second, your child will learn that word parts have important meanings.

Working with compound words is a wonderful way to help your child build self-esteem and confidence in reading. Why? Many times intermediate-level readers will have no problem with short one-syllable words, but will give up quickly or stumble on longer words. Compound words are really big words that your child will actually be able to read independently with very little instruction. If your child can read a one-syllable word, he or she can read a compound word. All you need to do is introduce the child to a strategy or a plan for reading compound words and provide a little practice. Learning to read compound words is a starting point for teaching your child to sound out more complicated words.

TEACHING TIPS

- ✓ Explain that a compound word is two smaller words that have been joined together. All the letters of both the smaller words are used: *mailman, goldfish,* and *footprint.*
- ✓ Tell your child to look for the first little word that is inside the compound word and then to read the last part of the word. Then say both parts of the word together.

CONFOUNDING COMPOUNDS

Read each compound word out loud to your parent. Tell your parent which two words have been joined to make the compound word. Then write the two little words on the lines below.

1. afternoon _____ _____

2. baseball _____ _____

3. catfish _____ _____

4. yourself _____ _____

5. upstairs _____ _____

6. waterfall _____ _____

7. landlady _____ _____

8. tattletale _____ _____

COMPOUND IT

Now, read these sentences and circle the compound words in each sentence. Ask your parent to check your work. How did you do? Beware! Some sentences have more than one compound word.

1. My goldfish lives in a bowl on the kitchen sink.

2. The weatherman's report for this weekend said it would be warm and sunny.

3. I like to watch the water form a whirlpool when it goes down the bathtub drain.

4. I had to walk downstairs when the doorbell rang.

5. My history homework accidentally fell into the wastebasket this morning.

6. The salesperson brought out three skateboards for me to choose from.

7. My dad and I found a starfish covered with seaweed lying on the beach.

8. The snowstorm hit the city very quickly. Everyone hurried inside.

On Your Own

CREATING COMPOUNDS

Read the following words out loud. Figure out which words can be put together to make compound words. On a separate sheet of paper, write the words that form compound words. Some words can be used more than once.

air	room	hand	lace	oat	set
in	down	arm	boat	lip	bolt
count	mail	neck	chair	wild	stick
your	to	row	tie	thunder	meal
class	self	cuffs	up	cat	man

IMAGINE THAT!

The word "ketchup" or "catsup" (both ways of spelling it are correct) is a combination of two words that used to mean "fish sauce." Now made from tomato sauce, Americans like ketchup so much each one of us eats three bottles of it every year!

COMPOUNDING SITUATION

Read each sentence and find two words from each sentence that will make a compound word. Write the compound word on the blank.

1. The light that is reflected off of the moon is called _____.

2. A coat that a person wears in the rain is called a _____.

3. A fish that has whiskers like a cat is called a _____.

4. A hole that is used for a key is called a _____.

5. A shell from an animal that lived in the sea is called a _____.

6. The days that come at the end of the week are called _____.

7. A pin that in used in a person's hair is called a _____.

8. A house that is made for a doll is called a _____.

9. An area of ground where people play is called a _____.

10. A light you leave on all night is called a

_____.

On the Go. . .

MAKING SENSE AND NONSENSE

Making up weird and wacky compound words is a fun way to get extra practice with compound words and their meanings. Call out a word (any word will do). Then have your child call out another word (it should be one that you can join to the first word, but it doesn't have to make sense). You then join the words together and call out the compound word that was formed. Then your child has to make up a definition for the newly invented compound word. For example, you call out "bird." Your child calls out "plucker." You then say, "birdplucker." Your child says, "It is a machine that plucks feathers from birds." Take turns being first in this game. The main idea is to have fun with words and to develop a firm understanding of compound-word meanings.

UNDERSTANDING CONTRACTIONS

Parents' Corner

Your child should now begin a level of reading development called word study, which focuses on word parts. A contraction is a one-word shortcut for writing two words. The first part of a contraction is almost always a whole word. The second part of a contraction is another word, but the word is incomplete—some of the letters are missing. An apostrophe is written to take the place of the missing letter or letters. Some examples of contractions include:

is or *has* examples	he's, here's, it's
am example	I'm
are examples	they're, we're, you're
have examples	could've, I've, might've
had, would examples	he'd, I'd, that'd
will examples	he'll, I'll, it'll
us example	let's
not examples	aren't, can't, couldn't

In standardized tests, your child will probably encounter contractions in subtests of either the language expression or language mechanics. Check out Prima's *Better Test-Taking in 5 Minutes a Day* for practice activities to improve both test-taking and writing. Tell your child how important it is to place the apostrophe between the correct letters when writing contractions. Remember, the apostrophe takes the place of the missing letter or letters.

TEACHING TIPS

✔ Teach your child to place the apostrophe between the correct letters when writing contractions.

✔ The first part of a contraction is almost always a whole word. The part after the apostrophe is always missing some letters.

✔ There is one exception that you need to explain to your child. The word *won't* is a special contraction made from the words *will* and *not*.

AT THE KITCHEN TABLE

CONTRACTION CONCENTRATION

This is a fun game to play with a friend, but before you can play you have to make some cards. Cut some heavy paper into 2 × 2 inch squares (or ask your parent if you can use some old business cards). You'll need about forty pieces of paper. On one card write a contraction. On another card write the two words that make up that contraction. When you have finished, you will have paper cards naming all the contractions you know and all of the word pairs that make up the contractions.

Mix up the cards, and place them face down. Choose two paper cards and turn them over. If the two cards chosen are a contraction and the pair of words that make up the contraction, they are a set. You get to keep the set and take another turn. If the cards don't match, put them back, facedown, exactly where you found them. Now it's your friend's turn. The trick is to concentrate and remember where each card is so you can turn up the matching answer the next time. The player with the most sets at the end of the game wins.

On Your Own

CONNECTING WITH CONTRACTIONS

You use contractions all the time when you talk. Now see if you can identify the two separate words that make up the contraction. Write the two words in the space provided next to the contraction. Ask your parent to check your answers or help you if you get stuck.

1. I'm _____

2. you'll _____

3. she's _____

4. we're _____

5. they'd _____

6. isn't _____

7. you're _____

8. he's _____

9. I've _____

10. let's _____

11. it'll _____

12. what's _____

13. won't _____

14. hasn't _____

15. this'll _____

16. don't _____

17. can't _____

18. mustn't _____

Now complete each sentence using a contraction from the contraction list above.

1. The teacher said, "_____ forget to bring back your permission slips."

2. My dog _____ jump over that fence. It's too high.

3. _____ a lot of homework to work on tonight.

4. _____ the matter with your cat? Why did you take it to the veterinarian?

5. The weatherman said _____ be warm and sunny tomorrow.

6. My sister is taking us to the zoo. Then _____ taking us to get some ice cream.

7. My friends said _____ come over to my house this weekend

8. If you look at the newspaper today, _____ find the President on the front page.

9. _____ quite proud of the project we are doing in school.

10. The coach said that _____ not worried about the team's chances in the playoffs.

11. There _____ been a winter with this much rain in more than fifty years.

12. The doctor said that I _____ scratch my chicken pox.

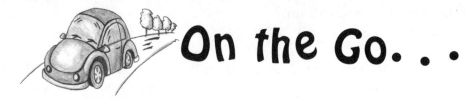

On the Go. . .

BEAT THE CLOCK

The next time you are out running errands, have your child hunt for contractions. See how many your child can find in five minutes. If you are driving down the road, your child can look on billboards or storefronts. If you are the dentist's office, look through magazines. If you are waiting in line at the checkout stand of a grocery store, look around at the display cases and magazine racks. Go for a world record! Make sure your child chooses contractions and not possessive words.

SIGHT WORDS AND CHECK-UP

Set Your Sights on These Sight Words

breathe	aisle	all	bold	allow
affect	because	alight	he'd	angle
clothesline	bear	close	ewe	foreword
fourteen	he'll	guest	gilt	hallway
friendship	lonesome	mankind	our	vary
otherwise	psychic	remove	sew	thoughtful
weird	tier	who's	whose	anywhere
waterfall	aye			

Compound Words and Contractions Check-Up

Have your child separate these compound words into the two words that make up each word.

1. birthdate _____ _____

2. cupboard _____ _____

3. laughingstock _____ _____

4. notebook _____ _____

5. lifeguard _____ _____

6. wristwatch _____ _____

7. roommate _____ _____

8. earthquake _____ _____

Now have your child turn the following into contractions. Remind your child to be careful where he or she places the apostrophe!

9. I will _____

10. she is _____

11. you would _____

12. you have _____

13. I am _____

14. I would _____

15. I have _____

16. he is _____

17. we have _____

18. let us _____

19. he would _____

20. they have _____

21. you are _____

22. she would _____

23. could have _____

24. we are _____

25. we would _____

26. would have _____

27. they are _____

28. they would _____

29. should have _____

30. who are _____

31. who would _____

32. might have _____

33. could not _____

34. can not _____

35. should not _____

36. will not _____

37. are not _____

38. does not _____

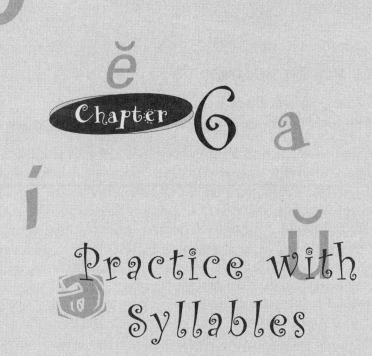

Chapter 6

Practice with Syllables

In This Chapter

SYLLABLE VOWEL SOUNDS

Parents' Corner

Once your child has learned to apply phonics skills to reading one-syllable words, he or she is ready for the logical next step: reading two-syllable words. Many intermediate-age students "freeze up" when they encounter words with more than one syllable. Their knowledge of phonics is critically important to help them with pronunciation, but reading two-syllable words requires more than just the knowledge of and ability to use phonics. Your child must also be able to break a complicated word into smaller, readable parts. Once your child begins to recognize these readable parts, doors will open to more difficult stories and more complex writing. Children's spelling and vocabulary will also improve significantly as they master the skills of syllabication.

Every syllable in every word has a vowel sound. Sometimes it is a long vowel sound, sometimes it is a short vowel sound, and sometimes it is a special vowel sound. When your child can determine the number of vowel sounds a word has, he or she will be able to determine the number of syllables in any word. Explain to your child that if you know how to break a word into syllables, or smaller pieces, you can sound out these word parts, and then read the whole word. In this lesson, your child will focus on identifying and counting the vowel sounds in words.

TEACHING TIPS

✓ Teach your child that syllables are word parts that have a vowel.

✓ Sometimes two or more letters can stand for a single vowel sound, as in easy, read, through, and rainbow.

✓ Have your child count the vowel sounds to find out how many syllables are in a word.

AT THE KiTCHEN TABLE

HOW MANY SYLLABLES CAN YOU SEE?

Can you find all the vowel sounds in these two- and three-syllable words? Read each word aloud and count the vowel sounds you hear. Then write down the number of syllables each word has. Remember that each syllable must have a vowel sound in it. Finally, write down the vowels for each syllable. Ask your parent to check your answers. The first one is done for you as an example.

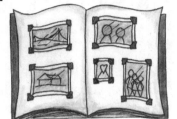

Say the Word	How Many Syllables?	What Are the Vowel Sound-Spellings?
wonderful	3	o, er, u
1. factory		
2. pendant		
3. focus		
4. literate		
5. reject		
6. pretending		
7. photograph		
8. divert		
9. system		

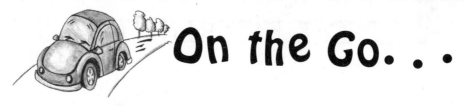

On the Go...

A SYLLABLE HUNT

Encourage your child to find words with many syllables. If you are away from home, your children can find words on road signs, billboards, menus, grocery items, or advertisements on the side of a bus. If you are doing chores around the house, your child can look on food labels, clothing, or book covers. See who can find the word with the most syllables. Refine the game by looking first for a one-syllable word, then look for a two-syllable word, next find a three-syllable word, and now find a four-syllable word. Who can find the word with the most syllables?

On Your Own

DON'T SKIP A NOTE

Using your favorite comic book, reading book, or magazine, start looking for words with many syllables. Make a list of the two-syllable words, three-syllable words, four-syllable words, and maybe even five-syllable words that you find in your favorite reading material. Do you already know how to read these words, or do you skip over them when you read because they are too hard? If you have been skipping over these words, just grit your teeth and decide that it's time to sound them out once and for all.

IMAGINE THAT!

Hippopotamonstrosisquepediliaphobia is the fear of large words. You sound it out like this: Hip-poh-pot-uh-mon-straw-sis-quip-ed-il-ee-yuh-foh-be-yuh.

SYLLABLE ACCENTS

Parents' Corner

An accented syllable is the part of the word that is stressed or empha-
sized when it is pronounced. Syllables that have less stress or emphasis are unaccented. When you sound out a word like *octopus*, it is
important to know which syllable to accent. If the accent is on the middle syllable, "to," the word would be pronounced like this (ok/toe/poos).
But in the word, the accent is actually on the first syllable, so it is pronounced like this (ok/tuh/poos). It is important to know which syllables are accented so that you pronounce the word correctly. This will
help your child recognize the meaning of the word. Also, because
unaccented syllables are often spelled with a vowel that is not pronounced, your child's spelling will improve once he or she masters this
skill.

Teach your child to listen to and count the number of syllables in
words by clapping the syllables as the word is pronounced. Slowly
read these words aloud *squash, sun-
shine, thirsty, mother, upon, turntable.* Have
your child tell you the number of syllables
in each word. Then have your child
repeat the word while clapping out
the syllables. Once your child is able to clap
out syllables accurately, ask him
or her to identify the accented
and unaccented syllables by clapping for
accented syllables and snapping for unaccented syllables.

TEACHING TIPS

✓ Teach your child to listen to and count the
number of syllables in words by clapping
and snapping.

✓ Certain syllables in words have more stress
or emphasis than others; these syllables are
accented (and clapped). Syllables that have
less stress or emphasis are unaccented (and
snapped).

✓ If your child isn't a good finger-snapper, slap
thighs for the unaccented syllables.

AT THE KITCHEN TABLE

CLAP AND COUNT

Read aloud and clap along with the following words. Count the number of syllables and write that number in the blank next to each word. Ask your parent to listen to you clap and count. Give yourself a big hand for good clapping.

1. bread _____

2. opposite _____

3. octopus _____

4. raining _____

5. under _____

6. however _____

7. pinstripe _____

8. selection _____

9. discover _____

10. stapler _____

11. generalize _____

12. fictional _____

SNAPPING AND CLAPPING

Now snap and clap along with the syllables in these words. Then circle the syllable that is accented (the one with the clap).

1. credit

2. convertible

3. import

4. inscribe

5. interrupt

6. faculty

7. eject

8. revert

9. adjective

On Your Own

A To Z Syllables

Look at magazines, advertisements, or newspapers and find a word with more than one syllable that begins with an "a." Say the word out loud while you snap and clap along with the syllables. Then, look for a "b" word and so on through all the letters of the alphabet. Give yourself extra credit if you find an "x" word!

IMAGINE THAT!

The longest one-syllable words in the English language have nine letters each. They are *straights, strengths,* and *screeched.*

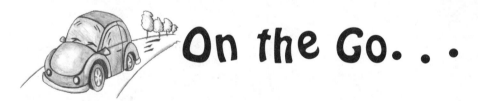

On the Go. . .

Silly Sentence Syllables

Take turns with your child making up silly sentences and ask your child to snap and clap for all the syllables in the sentence. Start with this one:

Green turtle soup looks like horrible goop!

You can even make this into a singing activity. The snapping and clapping will add rhythm to your new, silly songs.

IS IT OPEN OR CLOSED?

Parents' Corner

If a person is able to determine whether a syllable is open or closed, he or she is much more likely to be able to decide if the vowel sounds are long or short. This skill will allow your child to figure out how to pronounce unknown words with remarkable accuracy. This concept is one of the easiest and most powerful methods for improving your child's ability to read words that have multiple syllables.

When breaking a word into smaller parts for reading, you must know the vowel's sound. Is it long or short? For example, in the word *baker* the "a" is found at the end of a syllable, and it makes the long vowel sound. This is called an open syllable. In the word *canter*, the "a" is in the middle of a syllable, and it makes a short vowel sound. This is called a closed syllable. Vowel sounds at the beginning of words also have short vowel sounds and are also called closed syllables.

Chapter 3 introduced the importance of developing reading flexibility. When reading unknown multisyllabic words, flexibility is very important. Your child needs to learn how to adjust the pronunciation of a word if the sound of the word doesn't make sense or to connect with a word that your child has heard before. If your child mispronounces a word, encourage him or her to try again, using an alternate vowel sound.

TEACHING TIPS

✔ Open syllables: If the vowel is at the end of a syllable, it is usually a long vowel sound such as in ba / ker, be / ing, and bro / ker.

✔ Closed syllables: If the vowel is not at the end of a syllable, it is usually a short vowel sound such as in can / ter, es / tab / lish, and tug / ging

AT THE KITCHEN TABLE

BUZZING ALONG THE OPEN MAZE

Your job is to help the bee get to his hive. Follow the path of open syllables. Draw a line to show the path the bee must follow, and avoid those closed syllables if you want to make it to the hive. Ask your parent for some help if you get lost in the maze.

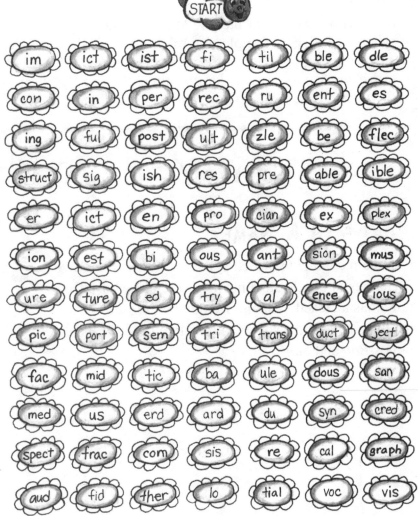

START

im	ict	ist	fi	til	ble	dle
con	in	per	rec	ru	ent	es
ing	ful	post	ult	zle	be	flec
struct	sig	ish	res	pre	able	ible
er	ict	en	pro	cian	ex	plex
ion	est	bi	ous	ant	sion	mus
ure	ture	ed	try	al	ence	ious
pic	port	sern	tri	trans	duct	ject
fac	mid	tic	ba	ule	dous	san
med	us	erd	ard	du	syn	cred
spect	trac	com	sis	re	cal	graph
aud	fid	ther	lo	tial	voc	vis

END

On the Go. . .

BACK TO BASICS

Start with a word that has the long *a* sound ending the first syllable of a two-syllable word. For example, you might use the word *ba / sic*. Take turns with your child thinking up more words with this sound until you both are stumped. Then move on to words with long *e*, then *i*, *o*, and *u*. Examples of each include *re / move*, *bi / cy / cle*, *clo / ser*, and *bu / tane*.

On Your Own

WHAT'S IN A NAME?

Practice recognizing closed syllables by writing down the names of all the students in your class whose first name has a closed syllable. Remember, closed syllables have short vowel sounds like those in the names *Bob* and *Sam*.

Just for Fun!
What is the longest word in the dictionary? Smiles—because there is a mile between each "S."

CONSONANT SYLLABLE DIVISION AND THE SCHWA

Parents' Corner

After your child has learned to identify the vowel sounds within a word, he or she needs to learn to break the word into syllables. The previous lesson taught your child how to recognize the number of syllables, but it did not teach exactly where the syllables were divided.

The easiest words to divide are those containing double consonants that follow a vowel. Show your child how to break a word into smaller parts, or syllables, by looking for two consonants that follow a vowel. Break the words between the two consonants, as in *smal / lest, shor / ter,* and *sub / tract.* Some multisyllabic words are rule-breakers, so if a word does not sound correct, try dividing it into different syllables. (Remember, some words cannot be sounded out.)

TEACHING TIPS

✓ Remind your child to snap accented syllables and clap unaccented syllables to help pronounce multisyllable words.

✓ Show your child how to divide syllables between two consonants that follow a vowel.

✓ The *uh* schwa sound usually appears in an unaccented (snap) syllable and is frequently a one-letter syllable.

Vowels in unaccented syllables make the schwa (ə) sound. The schwa sound is like the short *u* in *duck,* but it can be represented by any of the vowels. The vowel "a" can sound like ə in *a / bout.* The vowel "e" can sound like short ə in *i / tem.* The vowel "i" can sound like ə in *ed / i / ble.* The vowel "o" can sound like ə in *gal / lop.* By recognizing the schwa sound, your child will be able to determine the unaccented syllables in a word.

AT THE KITCHEN TABLE

DIVIDE AND CONQUER!

Read the following words aloud to your parent, and snap and clap along with the syllables. Then write each word and draw a line (/) between its syllables. The first one is done for you.

1. sunlight   <u>sun / light</u>   **2.** mother   _____

3. postal   _____   **4.** standard   _____

5. jumping   _____   **6.** slowly   _____

7. winter   _____   **8.** cannot   _____

9. simple   _____   **10.** manner   _____

11. outward   _____   **12.** compress   _____

SNAPPY SYLLABLES

Say these schwa words aloud to your parent while you snap and clap along with the syllables. Then write each word and draw a line (/) between its syllables. Finally, circle the letter(s) that make the schwa sound.

1. formula _____   **2.** specimen _____

3. alfalfa _____   **4.** elephant _____

5. immigrant _____   **6.** ahead _____

7. allow _____   **8.** predicate _____

9. attitude _____   **10.** select _____

11. collect _____   **12.** agree _____

13. important _____   **14.** silliness _____

On Your Own

SPOT THE SCHWA!

Practice recognizing the schwa syllable in words by looking for words in newspapers and magazines that have more than one syllable. On a piece of paper, write each word that you find. Divide the words into syllables and circle the vowels that make the schwa sound. Remember, in a schwa syllable, the vowel makes the short *u* sound. Were you able to find schwa syllables for all of the vowels?

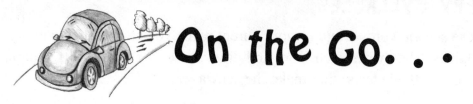

On the Go. . .

CAR PARTS, WORD PARTS

On your next trip in the car, have your child find as many inside car parts as he or she can with two consonants that follow a vowel. Ask your child to say each car part aloud and clap and snap along with the word parts (syllables). Here is one to get you started: *dash / board*. After you have found all the words, change the game by looking for car parts with a schwa word part, such as *antenna*.

SIGHT SYLLABLES, SIGHT WORDS, AND CHECK-UP

Set Your Sights on These Sight Syllables

in	im	ict	ist	er	ile	ble
dle	gle	zle	per	rec	ed	ent
ing	re	pre	post	ly	in	be
es	ize	pro	ish	ry	ity	able
ible	tri	ty	en	ict	ity	ey
lly	ion	est	ure	ous	ant	ate
mus	al	ture	ive	acc	bio	ence
iour	ory	try	semi	ar	sym	syn
ogy	psy	mid	tice	ex	cred	dous
fac	pic	us	struct	sive	trans	duct
ject	spect	trac	con	struct	flec	tic
graph	aud	try	ther	sub	cial	fect

Set Your Sights on These Sight Words

among	any	blood	break	busy
calf	clothes	cough	debt	doubt
February	floor	gone	guy	guard
guess	guide	height	honest	iron
lose	island	listen	eye	laugh
live	month	muscle	ninth	ocean
pint	pretty	push	rough	steak
sugar	touch	truth	wind	wolf

Syllable Check-Up

Have your child read the syllables below. Work with your child to combine the syllables into words. Have your child write the words on a separate sheet of paper. Syllables may be used more than once. Challenge your child to build words with more than two syllables from this list.

pic	ict	list	pre	tion	ing	walk
sing	write	ful	er	join	peti	un
play	ture	ible	able	re	en	green
ig	call	nore	speak	ant	sigh	ad
work	just	act	con	ly	or	duct

Chapter 7

Prefixes and Suffixes

In This Chapter

PERFECTING PREFIXES

Parents' Corner

Prefixes are special word parts that are added to the beginning of words to change the meaning of base words. The base word is the word part that carries the basic meaning of the word. Therefore, your child needs to fully understand not only the meaning of the prefix but also how a prefix changes the meaning of the base word. For example, in the word *preview*, the prefix "pre" means "before" and the base word "view" means "to see." Thus, *preview* means "to see before."

The activities in this lesson will give your child an understanding of how prefixes change the meaning of words and how they can be used to break a word into smaller, easier-to-read word parts. Explain that words can be broken down into syllables by dividing the word between the prefix and the base word. This makes the words easier to read and understand. Automatic recognition of prefixes as readable syllables will help your child pronounce difficult words when reading, to spell difficult words when writing, and to understand the meaning of the words. Understanding the meaning of the most common prefixes will also provide clues to meaning of unknown words. Using knowledge of prefixes, along with other context clues, can significantly improve reading vocabulary.

TEACHING TIPS

✔ Make prefix flashcards and practice often.

✔ Help your child make a memory picture of each prefix. Have your child study the word, close his or her eyes and picture the word, say the definition and spelling, then open his or her eyes to check for accuracy.

✔ Remind your child to note how the prefix changes the meaning of the attached base word.

AT THE KITCHEN TABLE

PICTURE THIS

Memorize the meanings and spellings of these prefixes that have to do with numbers. Make flash cards from index cards, Post-it Notes, or old business cards to help you memorize. Ask your parent to quiz you once you think you know them all.

Prefix	Meaning	Example
uni-	one	unicorn (one horn)
bi-	two	biplane (plane with two wings)
tri-	three	triangle (three angles)
centi-	hundredth	centimeter (one-hundredth of a meter)
cent-	hundred	century (one hundred years)

Now read these sentences and the clues below each line and write in the missing prefix that completes the sentence.

1. When I went to the circus I saw a man riding a(n) _____cycle on a
   tightrope.   one

2. The newspaper reported that Ms. Smith had _____plets last
   Saturday.   three

3. Today's temperature should reach the _____ury mark on the weather
   thermometer.   hundred

4. The United Stated celebrated its _____ _____ennial in 1996.
                                         two hundred

5. An optometrist prescribed _____focal glasses for Lee.
                                    two

6. My little brother was given a new _____cycle for his birthday.
                                          three

7. All the students at my elementary school wear a school _____form.
                                                              one

8. A(n) _____meter is a metric unit of length.
      hundredth

SYLLABLE AND WORD LIST

Match the number prefixes with the words and syllables listed here to make bigger words that match the clues. You may need to use some word parts more than once.

annual	cycle	weekly	plane	angle
meter	sect	lingual	ped	ennial

1. occurring twice a year _____

2. three-wheeled bike _____

3. one-wheeled bike _____

4. two-winged plane _____

5. three angled shape _____

6. 1/100th of a meter _____

7. speaking or singing together _____

8. a mythical horse with one horn _____

9. to divide in two _____

10. able to use two languages _____

11. a two-footed animal _____

OPPOSITES AND NONSENSE

Memorize the meanings and spellings of these prefixes that have to do with negatives. Make your flash cards and practice. Ask your parent to quiz you when you are ready.

Prefix	Meaning	Example
dis	not or opposite	dislike (not like)
un	not	unhappy (not happy)
non	not	nonliving (not living)
mis	badly, wrongly	mistreat (treat badly) opposite

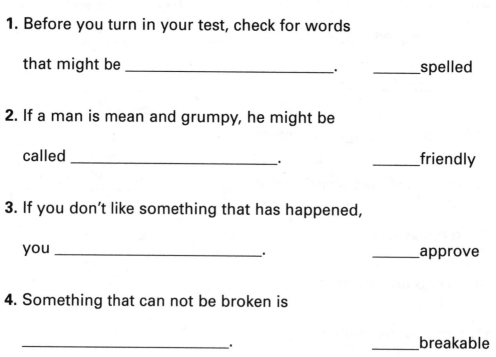

Read the sentences below, and figure out if you should add a "dis," "un," "mis," or "non" to the words to the right to complete the sentence. Write the entire word on the blank in the sentence, and have your parent check to be sure that you spelled it correctly.

1. Before you turn in your test, check for words

that might be _____.   _____spelled

2. If a man is mean and grumpy, he might be

called _____.   _____friendly

3. If you don't like something that has happened,

you _____.   _____approve

4. Something that can not be broken is

_____.   _____breakable

5. A _____ book is written
to tell facts about something.   _____fiction

6. Something that is not organized may be called

_____   _____orderly

7. If you are sad, you are _____. _____happy

8. The spoiled milk had a(n)

_____ smell.   _____pleasant

9. You should never _____
your pets.   _____treat

10. If you don't know about something, you are

_____ of it.   _____aware

11. A magician's favorite trick is to make things

_____   _____appear

12. The dog was _____ to
climb over the fence.   _____able

13. To judge someone wrongly, is to

_____   _____judge

ROOT OUT THE ROOT WORD

Each of the following words has a prefix. Separate the prefix from the root word (the part of the word that carries the meaning of the word) and write each in the blanks provided.

Word	Prefix	Root Word
1. dislike	_____	_____
2. rewrite	_____	_____
3. prediction	_____	_____
4. posttest	_____	_____
5. misdirect	_____	_____
6. reusable	_____	_____
7. distrust	_____	_____
8. unwrap	_____	_____
9. midnight	_____	_____
10. midyear	_____	_____
11. preheat	_____	_____

On Your Own

ARE YOU PREPARED?

Memorize the meanings and spellings of these prefixes that have to do with time. Make and practice flash cards for these word parts.

Prefix	Meaning	Example
pre	before	prepay (pay before)
post	after	postwar (after the war)
re	again	repaint (paint again)
mid	middle or half	midway (half of the way)

Read each of these sentences and the words beside them. Add "re" or "post" to the word and write it down to complete each sentence.

1. The pilot wrote the _____ report. _____flight

2. The sports commentator played a

_____ of the touchdown. _____play

3. Many members of the team were at

the _____ party. _____game

4. The police officer had to _____
the traffic after the accident. _____direct

5. In many social studies classes students

discuss _____ life.   _____war

6. Some models of cars have a good

_____ value.   _____sale

In the next six sentences add "pre" or "mid" to the word and write it in the blank to complete each sentence.

7. At _____ we stopped to
eat a picnic lunch by the lake.   _____day

8. My sister and I went to see the

_____ of the new movie.   _____view

9. My uncle's farm is located in the

_____.   _____west

10. I always forget to _____
the oven when I am baking a cake.   _____heat

11. At some gas stations you have to   _____pay

_____ for the gas.

WHO KNOWS WHAT I MEAN?

Write the prefix for each word on this list on the line beside the word. Write the meaning of each prefix in the middle column. Then write the meaning of the whole word in the last column. The first one is done for you as an example. Be sure to check your work. Is the meaning clear to you now?

Word	Prefix	Prefix Meaning	Word Meaning
prepay	pre	before	to pay before
1. rewrite	_____	_____	_____
2. postgame	_____	_____	_____
3. midwest	_____	_____	_____
4. postwar	_____	_____	_____
5. midnight	_____	_____	_____
6. prejudge	_____	_____	_____
7. reevaluate	_____	_____	_____

TRICOLOR PREFIX LOOK-OUT

Find a large piece of paper and three different-colored pens. You can cut open a grocery bag if you don't have any large paper at home. Save and use the same paper for a couple of weeks. Every time you read a book, newspaper, magazine, or schoolwork, take a few extra minutes to write down in one color any words that have the prefixes you have learned in this lesson. Then, write the prefix of each word in a second color, and finally, write the meaning of the word, as used in the reading, in a third color.

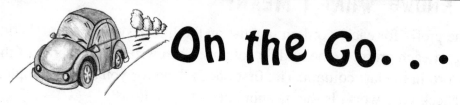

On the Go. . .

A PREFIX PARTY

In the car, or wherever you are, practice prefixes with your child. Here is one game idea. Pick a prefix and have your child come up with an example word using that word part. Then you come up with another example. Continue until one of you runs out of example words. The "loser" thinks of and says the next prefix and the "winner" has to give the first example.

SUFFIXES FOR SUCCESS

Parents' Corner

A suffix is a letter or group of letters that can be added to the end of a word. Learning about suffixes can be more difficult than learning about prefixes because, unlike prefixes, suffixes may change the spelling of the base word when they are added. In addition, many different suffixes have similar meanings. Frequently, suffixes do not provide any significant meaning to the word; instead they simply change the part of speech.

When your child is learning new suffixes, you can help by asking him or her to say the base word and the meaning of the suffix together, and then say them again in a reversed order. For example, if the word is *restful*, your child would say, "Rest—full of or having;" then "full of or having—rest." This will help your child gain a better understanding of how a suffix changes the meaning of a base word.

The suffixes in these activities are probably familiar to you and your child, but remembering the meanings for many new suffixes can be confusing. Take as much time as you need to guarantee that your child understands the uses and meanings these suffixes. It will help your child become a more successful reader and a more sophisticated writer.

TEACHING TIPS

✓ A suffix is a word part added on to the end of a word and that some words may have more than one suffix, or may have both suffixes and prefixes.

✓ Help your child make a memory picture of each of these suffixes.

✓ Remind your child to note how some suffixes can change the meaning of the attached base word and that the base word spelling may change when the suffix is added.

AT THE KITCHEN TABLE

ADD A "TAIL" OF YOUR OWN

Memorize the meanings and spellings of these suffixes. Ask your parent to check you out when you think have learned them all.

Suffix	Meaning	Example
-y	having or tending to	muddy (having mud)
-ly	in a way that is like	calmly (in a calm way)
	every	yearly (every year)
-ful	full of or having	restful (full of rest)
-less	without	waterless (without water)

Now complete these sentences by adding "y," "ly," "ful," or "less" to the word on the blank line. Read each sentence aloud to your parent to be sure it makes sense.

1. The pitcher calm_____ walked to the mound.

2. Papa's injury was a pain_____ reminder of the accident that occurred several months ago.

3. The old house creaked and moaned due to the storm_____ night.

4. Tofu is a white flavor_____ food that my mom uses to make fruit shakes.

5. There is nothing I like better on a hot day, than a frost_____ mug of ice-cold root beer.

6. In the 4th grade I had to complete month_____ book reports.

7. I rare_____ fall when I go ice skating, but last week I fell and bruised both my knees.

8. The next time I go skating I will be more care_____.

9. I saw a sign last week that advertised a water_____ car wash. I wonder how it works?

10. The last time I went to the movies, the popcorn was too salt_____.

11. My fifth grade teacher is wonder_____, but she is a little weird. And she looks a little bit like Mrs. Frizzle from the book, *The Magic School Bus.*

12. It was a joy_____ ride to the vet, because we were expecting to hear bad news.

13. My family's trip to the snow was real_____ fun. We are going back next weekend.

14. Our dog is nearly sight_____. She barks at everything.

15. After driving on a dirt road, the car was quite dust_____.

16. My son's first truck was old, but it had a power_____ engine.

HANGING OUT IN THE HOOD

Memorize the meanings and spellings of these suffixes. When you are ready, ask your parent to quiz you on them. Did you get them all correct?

Suffix	Meaning	Example
-hood	state of being or condition	parenthood (state of being a parent)
-ish	like or somewhat	greenish (somewhat green)
-ness	state of being or condition	closeness (the condition of being close)
-able	can be or able to be	reachable (can be reached)

Now, read the words in the first column below. Circle the letters that form the suffix in each word. Then write the suffix in the second column. In the third column, write the base word. The first one has been done for you as an example.

Word	Suffix	Base word
1. boyhood	hood	boy
2. greenish		
3. closeness		
4. breakable		
5. childhood		
6. selfish		
7. sadness		

On Your Own

MY NEIGHBORHOOD

Write a short story about your neighborhood. Use lots of word with suffixes, including "hood," "ish," "ness," and "able." Be creative. Once you have finished writing your story, circle all the suffixes you have included.

TYING UP LOOSE ENDS

Memorize the meanings and spellings of these suffixes.

Suffix	Meaning	Example
-tion	condition or state of being	action (condition of acting)
-sion	condition or state of being	tension (state of being tense)
-ation	condition of state of being	beautification (state of being beautified)
-ist	one who makes or does	purist (one who makes pure)
-or	a person who or a thing that	estimator (a person who estimates)

Now complete each of these sentences with a word that ends with the suffix "sion," "tion," "ation," "ist," or "or." Then read the sentences aloud.

1. A person who invents is an _____.

2. Something that explains the answer is an

_____.

3. A person who acts is an _____.

4. A person who plays the violin is a _____.

5. An elected official in charge of governing a state is called a

_____.

6. A person who sculpts with clay is called a _____.

7. A place where something is located is called its _____.

8. When one automobile collides with another, it is called

a _____.

9. If an injury becomes infected it is called an

_____.

10. When a stick of dynamite explodes, it is called an

_____.

WORD SEARCH

Here are some words that don't have a home of their own. See if you can match each word to one of the sentences below.

tourist   governor   confusion
continuation   decision   explosion
collections   guitarist   exhibitor

1. My older sister is intensely protective of her coin and doll

    _____.

2. I carefully weighed all the facts before making my final

    _____.

3. The computer error at the airport caused a great deal of

    _____.

4. The residents of our state have elected a new

    _____.

5. Some businesses depend heavily on the

    _____ season.

6. The doctor recommended the _____ of physical therapy his patient.

7. Last year there was a(n) _____ at the asphalt company in Elk Grove.

8. There is a terrific _____ in my brother's band.

9. The art gallery is looking for a new _____.

TRICOLOR SUFFIX LOOK-OUT

Earlier in this chapter, you completed an activity that kept track of all the prefixes you read. It is time to do this activity again, but this time write down all of the suffixes you find in your reading.

Find a large piece of paper and three different colored pens. You can cut open a grocery bag if you don't have any large paper at home. For this activity, you are going to save and use the same large piece of paper for a couple of weeks. Every time you read, take a few extra minutes to write down in one color any words having the suffixes that you learned in this lesson. Then, write the suffix of each word in a second color. Finally, write the meaning of the word, as used in the reading, in a third color. Before long you will have filled your paper with suffixes!

On the Go. . .

SUFFIX SCRAMBLE

While you and your child are on the go, you can practice suffixes together. Choose a suffix and add it to anything and everything you see within one minute while your child counts the numbers of words. Now your child picks another suffix and repeats the process for one minute while you count. For example, if you chose "er," you might add it to the *turn* you see on a "No Left Turn" sign. Have fun with this. Make up new, funny words and try to come up with definitions for your new words.

SIGHT WORDS AND CHECK-UP

Set Your Sights on These New Words with Prefixes and Suffixes

introduction	literature	competence
rupture	structure	spectator
exclusively	convention	professor
cooperate	observant	information
destructive	extracted	midway
distaste	unintentional	reflective
conversion	convertible	detention
transformation	corrupted	subtraction
prescription	bilateral	destruction
diversion	decisive	rejected
interjection	conjunction	adjective
inductive	spectacular	gustatory
antiquated	incredulous	cooperation
respectfully	interdependence	inaudible
postpone	intentional	stupendous
manufactured	Dictaphone	

Set Your Sights on These New Multisyllable Sight Words

hippopotamus	chronometer	octagon	government
phonograph	monorail	pentathlon	moisture
accumulation	dermatology	orthodontist	biosphere
reconstructionist	illustrious	geometry	ophthalmoscope
cantankerous	blunderbuss	hyperactive	autobiography
metropolitan	architecture	microscope	microcosm
sympathetic	disturbance	devotion	thunderhead
psychologist	semicircle	symphonic	bibliography
incongruous	flamboyant	cantankerous	surrounding
dangerous	understandable	inventory	arduous

Prefixes and Suffixes Check-Up

Read the words and ask your child if each word has a prefix, a suffix, or both. Then have your child write the prefix and/or suffix and the meaning of each prefix or suffix on the lines beside each word.

Word	Prefix	Prefix Meaning	Suffix	Suffix Meaning
1. collection	_____	_____	_____	_____
2. rewrite	_____	_____	_____	_____
3. unhappiness	_____	_____	_____	_____
4. distasteful	_____	_____	_____	_____
5. precaution	_____	_____	_____	_____
6. prediction	_____	_____	_____	_____
7. guitarist	_____	_____	_____	_____
8. boyhood	_____	_____	_____	_____
9. restlessly	_____	_____	_____	_____
10. muddy	_____	_____	_____	_____
11. reaction	_____	_____	_____	_____
12. centimeter	_____	_____	_____	_____
13. uniforms	_____	_____	_____	_____
14. midsize	_____	_____	_____	_____
15. postwar	_____	_____	_____	_____

Answers

Chapter 1

Ready, Set, Review, p. 9
1. bat; 2. hen; 3. win; 4. dog; 5. cub; 6. tap; 7. net; 8. pig; 9. knock; 10. run; 11. pan; 12. belt; 13. swim; 14. pot; 15. tub
Things You Can Do: win, knock, pan, belt, run, swim, tap, bat
Kinds of Animals: bat, hen, cub, pig, dog
Things you can use: net, pan, belt, pot, tub, bat, tap

Sense or Nonsense?, pp. 12–13
1. brush; 2. watch; 3. thin; 4. chopped; 5. bath; 6. bench; 7. thick; 8. wheel; 9. shut; 10. peach

When Two Vowels Go Walking . . ., p. 16
Short vowel sounds: cut, strap, twist, quit, flat, split, frog, muck
Long vowel sounds: stove, twice, flute, plane, write, here, phone, slice

Back-to-Basics Check-Up, pp. 21–22

Word	Short Vowel	Final "e"	Consonant Pair	Soft "c"/"g"	Hard "c"/"g"	Sight Word
fad	✓					
less	✓					
clop	✓					✓
great					✓	✓
gust	✓		✓		✓	
skill	✓					
stack	✓		✓			
globe		✓			✓	
whole		✓			✓	
blend	✓		✓			
crept	✓		✓		✓	
till	✓					
stuff	✓					
male		✓				
plume		✓				
female		✓				
would						✓
smog	✓				✓	

Word	Short Vowel	Final "e"	Consonant Pair	Soft "c"/"g"	Hard "c"/"g"	Sight Word
gift	✓				✓	
grin	✓				✓	
tank	✓					
jig	✓			✓	✓	
space		✓		✓		
cage		✓		✓		
crisp	✓				✓	
slag	✓				✓	
face		✓		✓		
smite		✓				
skid	✓					
yell	✓					
scale		✓			✓	
price		✓		✓		
flop	✓					
grip	✓				✓	
mix	✓					
pole		✓				
give	✓	✓			✓	
scads	✓				✓	
pod	✓					
hunt	✓					

Chapter 2

Mix and Match, pp. 25–26

1. bird; 2. fern; 3. letter; 4. lantern; 5. curb; 6. shirt; 7. burn; 8. stir; 9. hurt; 10. whirl; 11. dirt; 12. furnace; 13. girl; 14. herd; 15. perfume; 16. purr; 17. turtle; 18. loafer; 19. circle; 20. perform

Are You Clued In?, pp. 29-30

1. p<u>or</u>k; 2. c<u>or</u>n; 3. sh<u>ar</u>k; 4. th<u>orn</u>; 5. c<u>ar</u>; 6. sh<u>ort</u>; 7. b<u>ark</u>; 8. sp<u>or</u>ts; 9. b<u>ar</u>n; 10. h<u>ar</u>d; 11. f<u>or</u>est; 12. sh<u>ar</u>p; 13. <u>or</u>ange; 14. f<u>ar</u>

Vowel Plus "r" Check-Up, pp. 32–33

1. Shirley; 2. her; 3. Harvey; 4. were; 5. porch; 6. were; 7. sorting; 8. storage; 9. corks; 10. forks; 11. sharp; 12. Shirley; 13. sharp; 14. dangerous; 15. father; 16. after; 17. Shirley; 18. her; 19. father; 20. Harvey; 21. mark; 22. sharp; 23. started; 24. mark; 25. another; 26. hurt; 27. arm; 28. sharp; 29. Father; 30. darted; 31. Harvey's; 32. Harvey; 33. blurted; 34. hurt; 35. arm; 36. Father; 37. nurse; 38. Father; 39. Harvey's; 40. arm; 41. worry; 42. Father; 43. smirked; 44. better; 45. Father; 46. Harvey; 47. Shirley; 48. grocery; 49. store

Chapter 3

Let's Sail on the Bay, pp. 36–37

ACROSS: 3. sail; 4. bait; 5. pay; 6. snail; 7. rain
DOWN: 1. maid; 2. clay; 3. stain; 4. bay; 6. stay

Let's Take a Sleigh Today, pp. 38–39

ACROSS: 3. eight; 4. sleigh; 5. cage; 7. chase
DOWN: 1. lake; 2. weight; 4. snake; 6. bake

Spill and Spell, pp. 42–44

1. soak; 2. blown; 3. goat; 4. roast; 5. boat; 6. mope; 7. hope; 8. coach; 9. plows; 10. show; 11. grown; 12. crow; 13. pillow; 14. floats

Give Me a High Five, p. 46

Long *i* Sound "ie" Spellings: dried, pie, tried, supplies, untie, flies, skies, fries, dies
Long *e* Sound "ie" Spellings: thief, niece, duties, grief, believe, stories, cities, berries, chief, pieces, cherries

Can You Tell This Story?, p. 47

1. night; 2. knight; 3. high; 4. light; 5. fright; 6. fight; 7. shield; 8. ride; 9. light; 10. five; 11. ride; 12. light; 13. quite; 14. relief; 15. knight; 16. light; 17. fire

The Unwanted Visitor, p. 49

mean, green, beast, near, fear, beast, sneak, eat, beast, steal, cream, beast, feast, sheep, creek, meeting, see, beast, team, weave, between, trees, creek, easily, seen, beast, creek, Three, beast, deep, beast

Want Ads, p. 52

Pets for Sale: cute, Poodle, soon, huge, usually, human, Sue, Hugh
Old Record Sale: new, music, mute, Few, good, used, to, Cube, super

The Long and Short of "y", p. 55
Long *e*: many, sticky, pretty, snowy, sunny, healthy, carry, nightly, soapy, turkey, celery, easy
Long *i*: why, cry, my, by, fly, pry, sky, dry, shy, spy, try, sly

Other Vowel Sounds Check-Up, pp. 57–58
1. bait; 2. snow; 3. melt; 4. blame; 5. greed; 6. choose; 7. way; 8. view; 9. know;
10. chief; 11. five; 12. loan; 13. plain; 14. use; 15. date
16. huge; 17. clean; 18. day; 19. nice; 20. white; 21. fright; 22. high; 23. sly; 24. light;
25. thief; 26. few; 27. sweet

Chapter 4

Ahoy to the Sound of oy, p. 61
1. enjoy; 2. voice; 3. boy; 4. noise; 5. coins; 6. toys; 7. soil; 8. spoiled

Oh Boy, More Practice!, pp. 62–63
1. oil; 2. boiled; 3. joined; 4. Toys; 5. noise; 6. disappoint; 7. choice; 8. hoist; 9. boiling;
10. noisy

The Wizard of Aaah's, pp. 66–67
1. sauce; 2. hawk; 3. caught; 4. pawn; 5. crawl; 6. faucet; 7. laundry; 8. straw; 9. launch

Aw Shucks, p. 67
1. paws; 2. fawn; 3. taunt; 4. lawn; 5. jaw; 6. auto; 7. claw

"oo" Challenge, p. 70
Short *oo* words: pudding, pushing, sugar
Long *oo* words: tutor, suit, tune, new, fluid, dude, stew, fruit, duty, flute, blew, juice, tube, duke, crew, cruise, clue, blue, shrew, dew, recruit, true, pursuit, glue, flew

Look for "oo" at High Noon, p. 71
Long *oo*: boot, broom, tooth, spoon, moose, food, spool, tools, snoop, goose, gloom, zoom, scoot
Short *oo*: hood, book, foot, wood, hook, shook, nook, hoof, stood, took, good

"ew," "ui," "oo," and "u_e" Check-Up, p. 73
1. dune; 2. chute; 3. shook; 4. croon; 5. brew; 6. look; 7. tune; 8. spool; 9. blue;
10. crook; 11. flue; 12. swoon; 13. stood; 14. suit; 15. cook

"au," "aw," "oi," and "oy" Check-Up, p. 74

1. launch; 2. sauce; 3. coins; 4, jaw 5. oily; 6. haul; 7. auto; 8. paws; 9. crawl; 10. claws; 11. loyal; 12. enjoyed; 13. boiling; 14. dawn; 15. boy; 16. point

Chapter 5

Confounding Compounds, p. 77

1. after, noon; 2. base, ball; 3. cat, fish; 4. your, self; 5. up, stairs; 6. water, fall; 7. land, lady; 8. tattle, tale

Compound It, p. 78

1. goldfish; 2. weatherman, weekend; 3. whirlpool, bathtub; 4. downstairs, doorbell; 5. homework, wastebasket; 6. salesperson, skateboards; 7. starfish, seaweed; 8. snowstorm, everyone

Creating Compounds, p. 79

Answers may include airmail, countdown, yourself, classroom, into, handcuffs, armchair, necktie, rowboat, necklace, oatmeal, lipstick, wildcat, thunderbolt, upset, handset, setup, inset, mailroom, necktie, stickup, mailman

Compounding Situation, p. 80

1. moonlight; 2. raincoat; 3. catfish; 4. keyhole; 5. seashell; 6. weekend; 7. hairpin; 8. dollhouse; 9. playground; 10. nightlight

Connecting with Contractions, pp. 83–85

Part 1: 1. I am; 2. you will; 3. she is; 4. we are; 5. they would or they had; 6. is not; 7. you are; 8. he is; 9. I have; 10. let us; 11. it will; 12. what is; 13. will not; 14. has not; 15. this will; 16. do not; 17. can not; 18. must not

Part 2: 1. don't; 2. can't or won't; 3. I've; 4. what's; 5. it'll; 6. she's; 7. they'd; 8. you'll; 9. I'm; 10. he's; 11. hasn't; 12. mustn't

Compound Words and Contractions Check-Up, pp. 87–88

1. birth, date; 2. cup, board; 3. laughing, stock; 4. note, book; 5. life, guard; 66. wrist, watch; 7. room, mate; 8. earth, quake; 9. I'll; 10. she's; 11. you'd; 12. you've; 13. I'm; 14. I'd; 15. I've; 16. he's; 17. we've; 18. let's; 19. he'd; 20. they've; 21. you're; 22. she'd; 23. could've; 24. we're; 25. we'd; 26. would've; 27. they're; 28. they'd; 29. should've; 30. who're; 31. who'd; 32. might've; 33. couldn't; 34. can't; 35. shouldn't; 36. won't; 37. aren't; 38. doesn't

Chapter 6

How Many Syllables Can You See?, p. 91
1. 3: a, or, y; 2. 2: e, a; 3. 2: o, u; 4. 3: i, er, a_e; 5. 2: e, e; 6. 3: e, e, i; 7. 3: o, o, a; 8. 2: i, er; 9. 2: y, e

Clap and Count, p. 94
1. 1 syllable; 2. 3 syllables; 3. 3 syllables; 4. 2 syllables; 5. 2 syllables; 6. 3 syllables; 7. 2 syllables; 8. 3 syllables; 9. 3 syllables; 10. 2 syllables; 11. 4 syllables; 12. 3 syllables

Snapping and Clapping, p. 94
1. <u>cred</u>it; 2. con<u>vert</u>ible; 3. <u>im</u>port; 4. in<u>scribe</u>; 5. inter<u>rupt</u>; 6. <u>fac</u>ulty; 7. e<u>ject</u>; 8. re<u>vert</u>; 9. <u>ad</u>jective

Buzzing Along the Open Maze, p. 97
START-fi-ru-be-pre-pro-bi-try-tri-ba-du-re-lo-END

Divide and Conquer!, p. 100
1. sun/light; 2. mo/ther; 3. post/al; 4. stan/dard; 5. jump/ing; 6. slow/ly; 7. wint/er; 8. can/not; 9. sim/ple; 10. man/ner; 11. out/ward; 12. com/press

Snappy Syllables, p. 101
1. for/mu/la; 2. spec/i/men; 3. al/fal/fa; 4. el/e/phant; 5. im/mi/grant; 6. a/head; 7. al/low; 8. pred/i/cate; 9 at/ti/tude; 10. sel/ect; 11. col/lect; 12. ag/ree; 13. im/por/tant; 14. sil/li/ness

Syllable Check-Up, p. 104
Answers may include picture, listing, listen, walking, walker, singing, singer, writing, writer, written, playful, ignore, joiner, player, caller, speaker, worker, joining, petition, unjust, playact, enable, workable, rewrite, rejoin, replay, recall, react, rely, enlist, enjoin, enact, greening, greener, calling, speaking, sighing, acting, working, justly, conductor, actor

Chapter 7

Picture This, pp. 107–108
1. uni; 2. tri; 3. cent; 4. bicent; 5. bi; 6. tri; 7. uni; 8. centi

Syllable and Word List, p. 109
1. biannual; 2. tricycle; 3. unicycle; 4. biplane; 5. triangle; 6. centimeter; 7. unison; 8. unicorn; 9. bisect; 10. bilingual; 11. biped

Opposites and Nonsense, pp. 110–111

1. misspelled; 2. unfriendly; 3. disapprove; 4. unbreakable; 5. nonfiction; 6. disorderly; 7. unhappy; 8. unpleasant; 9. mistreat; 10. unaware; 11. disappear; 12. unable; 13. misjudge

Root Out the Root Word, p. 112

1. dis, like; 2. re, write; 3. pre, diction; 4. post, test; 5. mis, direct; 6. re, usable; 7. dis, trust; 8. un, wrap; 9. mid, night; 10. mid, year; 11. pre, heat

Are You Prepared?, pp. 113–114

1. postflight; 2. replay; 3. postgame; 4. redirect; 5. postwar; 6. resale; 7. midday; 8. preview; 9. midwest; 10. preheat; 11. prepay

Who Knows What I Mean?, p. 115

1. re, again, to write again; 2. post, after, after the game; 3. mid, middle, middle of the west; 4. post, after, after the war; 5. mid, middle, middle of the night; 6. pre, before, to judge before; 7. re, again, to evaluate again

Add a "Tail" of Your Own, pp. 118–119

1. calmly; 2. painful; 3. stormy; 4. tasteless; 5. frosty; 6. monthly; 7. rarely; 8. careful; 9. waterless; 10. salty; 11. wonderful; 12. joyless; 13. really; 14. sightless; 15. dusty; 16. powerful

Hanging Out in the Hood, p. 120

1. hood, boy; 2. ish, green; 3. ness, close; 4. able, break; 5. hood, child; 6. ish, self; 7. ness, sad

Tying Up Loose Ends, pp. 121–122

1. inventor; 2. explanation; 3. actor; 4. violinist; 5. governor; 6. sculptor; 7. location; 8. collision; 9. infection; 10. explosion

Word Search, p. 123

1. collection; 2. decision; 3. confusion; 4. governor; 5. tourist; 6. continuation; 7. explosion; 8. guitarist; 9. exhibitor

Prefixes and Suffixes Check-Up, p. 126

1. suffix: tion, state of being
2. prefix: re, again
3. prefix: un, not; suffix: ness, condition
4. prefix: dis, not; suffix: ful, having
5. prefix: pre, before; suffix: tion, condition
6. prefix: pre, before; suffix: tion, condition
7. suffix: ist, person who does
8. suffix: hood, condition
9. suffix: less, without; suffix: ly, like
10. suffix: y, having
11. prefix: re, again; suffix: tion, state of being
12. prefix: centi, hundredth
13. prefix: uni, one
14. prefix: mid, middle
15. prefix: post, after

Index